THE COMPANY WE KEEP

ADVANCE PRAISE

'Divya Khanna's *The Company We Keep* will find an important place in the emerging streams of thought and literature that are increasingly becoming the foundation for cultural transition in the post-pandemic era. Addressing the most important questions within organizations, its strength is the rich research base and the discourse with a vast array of people representing reality. Its purposeful narrative reveals the emotional dilemma, the conundrum of aspiration and the everyday battles that pave the path to a successful career. I am happy I got to read this book and got some interesting takeaways from it.'

Harsh Goenka
Chairman, RPG Enterprises

'In the era of Great Resignations and Quiet Quitting, Divya's book is a timely reminder for all corporates to look at their culture more closely. Consequences of corporate culture can be catastrophic for personal dignity and self-confidence. But it can be carefully crafted and changed for the positive with deliberate action. The authenticity of the book stems from the fact that its dominant insights come from personal experiences of Divya. I am sure it will be inspiring many a change!'

Dr Santrupt Misra
Group Director at Birla Carbon and Director Chemicals/Director Group HR at the Aditya Birla Group

'*The Company We Keep* is a timely book as people are figuring out their lives and careers in the new world post COVID-19. I have always believed that work-life balance is a must, but I know this is not the norm with younger people. Careers are important and you must have passion and work hard, but money alone doesn't make you feel like a true success.'

Aditya Puri
Senior Advisor at The Carlyle Group, ex-MD of HDFC Bank

'Things that bother young people are different from those that bother older people. Young people are not crazy. It is the old people who have forgotten how they were several years ago.

Ms Divya Khanna has stepped into this gap, very tastefully and artfully. This book is a valuable addition to readers who think.'

R. Gopalakrishnan
Author and Business Commentator

'A company is known for its culture—often the differentiating factor between a "good" company and one that is "great". At the dawn of a new post-pandemic era, we have seen a paradigm shift in this "culture", with "hybrid" working blurring the lines between personal and professional. Divya Khanna's book *The Company We Keep* thus comes at the right time when we need to re-evaluate our work and life choices to attain a balance that is not only humane but also productive.

Divya's effortless writing style, in-depth research and intriguing observations about corporate culture pushes the reader to introspect. This is a book that every corporate individual would relate to—be it an aspiring newbie, a hustling mid-level manager or even a seasoned leader.'

Sanjiv Mehta
CEO and Managing Director of Hindustan Unilever Limited, President at Unilever South Asia and Member of Unilever Leader Executive (Global Executive Board)

'The timing of Divya's book is serendipitous. Conceived before the pandemic, its relevance has increased manifold in today's context, when not only the nature of work is undergoing unimaginable churn but also the shapes of careers and people's life choices. Divya seamlessly weaves in stories, research and expert opinion to produce a valuable work that will be helpful for those navigating their careers through the maze of ambiguity and uncertainty as well as [for] senior leaders and HR professionals tasked with reengineering organisations in a post-COVID world. It will resonate as much with corporate mavericks like me as it would with hard-nosed careerists out to conquer the next peak.'

Sandip Ghose
Pioneering 'Corporate Quiet Quitter'
turned Media Commentator on Current Affairs

'Khanna has touched a chord with the topic of her book (an extremely relevant topic) more so on the back of the Pandemic, which has us all dwelling on what is most important to us. As Khanna so aptly puts it "life may never be the same"—in many ways, her book too will change the reader's worldview and work or the "work culture" may never seem the same.

I am most impressed by the combination of her understanding of culture and the impact that collective behaviour can have within a work environment and the objectivity and research behind her hypothesis and, most of all, the wonderful (predictable and yet unpredictable) conclusion that there are indeed no "easy answers" . . .

But on the other hand, her discovery that free choice indeed does exist and in fact it is in exercising that very right and the right to our "feelings" that leads us to the answer on how (or why) to impact our work culture or to fight it or even reject it to seek balance in our lives.'

Harshbeena Zaveri
VC and Managing Director, NRB Bearings Ltd.

'Are you feeling trapped in your job? Are you plagued by doubts that the shortcoming is yours? Or do you blame it all on toxic corporate culture and [are] taking a relook at your career? In this timely and relevant book, Divya Khanna analyses both the complexities of the modern workplace as well as the new changed employee, whose behaviour, priorities [and] career and life choices are very different. Although conceived before COVID-19 hit the world, the book is almost serendipitous as post pandemic, people have opened up about the burnout they feel, called out practices like bullying, discrimination and gender stereotyping at the workplace and the dissonance they feel with their managers. Divya has tackled all these issues, through her own candid personal account, extensive research—stories and surveys—as well as expert opinion. As you read the book, which perceptively lays bare the feelings of people, you will find yourself nodding in agreement and [will] no longer feel alone. For organizations, and especially human resource professionals, this book offers a path to understand the new employee and do course correction to make the workplace a happy one.'

Chitra Narayanan
Editorial Consultant, *The Hindu Business Line*,
and Author of *From Oberoi to Oyo*

'When Divya sent me a brief introduction about the book that she was writing, I was immediately reminded of a poignant "doha" (couplet) of Kabir.

> कस्तूरी कुँडल बसै, मृग ढ़ुढ़े बन माहिँ।
> ऐसे घटि घटि राम हैं, दुनिया देखे नाहिँ॥

Most of us spend a fortune in time and money gaining insight into others. This is true of individuals and organizations alike. However, introspection is given least importance and attention. This avoidance is probably driven by the fear of discovering something that is contrary to what we believe about ourselves. And having discovered it, it can be equally embarrassing and difficult to deal with.

Introspection need not necessarily be about discovering flaws. It could equally be about discovering one's strengths and the true potential. It is simpler to build on one's existing strength than create newer capabilities.

This book encourages looking at the mirror, celebrating the good looks and touching up the scars! I am sure that those interested in self-improvement would find it a fascinating and useful book to read [and] ruminate and act on.'

Ashok Barat
Corporate Advisor & Board Member,
Past President of Bombay Chamber of Commerce

'In the world plagued with uncertainty, volatility and ambiguity and extreme changes, are you concerned about your life, career, office politics, WHF, managing your boss, getting along with people and more?

Then *The Company We Keep: Insights into Indian Corporate Culture*, by Divya Khanna, will give you directions on how to navigate this onerous world.

Written in an easy-to-read style, it is laced with examples drawn from Divya Khanna's—herself a corporate warrior of yore—life and career as well as insights gleaned through scientific market research, [acquired] by speaking to people of eminence. This makes the content authentic, relatable and reliable. It is a must read for corporate warriors who are desirous of achieving a work-life balance and having a fulfilling corporate career.'

Rajesh Srivastava
Former CEO JK Helene Curtis, Adjunct Faculty IIM Indore (2008-2015), Author of Penguin bestsellers *The New Rules of Business* and *The 10 New Life-changing Skills*

'A must read for all professionals who want to lead an authentic life and find success and meaning in our fast-changing, complex and competitive world. This book is a rich resource for both descriptive scenarios and prescriptive formulas for the issues we face.'

Akhil Gupta
Former Chairman of Blackstone India

'This book is a very refreshing take on the corporate culture in our country. Divya has used her decades long experience in marketing to look at our corporate culture from a sociological perspective, with an interesting study on how our corporate culture is being shaped by many forces and the impact it is having on people. There are great insights in this book for leaders and organizations, as well as for those setting out to join the corporate world.'

Krish Shankar
Executive Vice President and Group Head, Human Resource Development, Infosys, and Author of *Catalyse*

'Analysing your career versus the corporate culture you work in can be a long battle. Divya's book can help you resolve some of these dilemmas. Read on!'

Piyush Pandey
Chief Creative Officer Worldwide and Executive Chairman India of Ogilvy

THE COMPANY WE KEEP

Insights into Indian Corporate Culture

DIVYA KHANNA

PENGUIN
VIKING
An imprint of Penguin Random House

VIKING

USA | Canada | UK | Ireland | Australia
New Zealand | India | South Africa | China

Viking is part of the Penguin Random House group of companies whose addresses can be found at global.penguinrandomhouse.com

Published by Penguin Random House India Pvt. Ltd
4th Floor, Capital Tower 1, MG Road,
Gurugram 122 002, Haryana, India

Penguin Random House India

First published in Viking by Penguin Random House India in 2023

10 9 8 7 6 5 4 3 2

The Company We Keep is based on the personal lived experiences of the author and the people who have participated in the research and surveys, data from which have been used in the book. The names and identifying details of these people have been changed to protect their privacy. The views and opinions expressed in this book are the author's own, the incidents related to her personal experiences are as have been narrated by her, the interviews and conversations reproduced herein are as have been narrated to the author and have been edited and condensed for clarity. Some of the subject matter of this book, based on the author's and select working professionals' experiences, relate to mental health matters stemming from work-induced stress, which include but might not be limited to mentions of anxiety and depression. These conversations reproduced herein between the author and the respondents should, in no way, be construed as medical advice. As such, reader discretion is advised. Penguin Random House is in no way liable for the same.

ISBN 9780670095797

Typeset in Adobe Caslon Pro by Manipal Technologies Limited, Manipal
Printed at Thomson Press India Ltd, New Delhi

www.penguin.co.in

MIX
Paper
FSC FSC® C010615

To all the corporate veterans, combatants and aspirants, to those confident of their corporate success and those struggling to make it, to those who have left in search of something different and to those who are on the cusp of critical career decisions and especially to my mamu and mami, Ashok and Kalyani Capoor, for modelling the balance that I aspire to achieve. As well as to my father, Uday Khanna, for inducting me into Indian corporate culture from a young age and for always being my safety net.

The Difficulty of Choice

We don't always know
The difference between:
Anchors and chains,
Free flight and free falling,
The roads taken and not,
What we want and what we need.
The choice is made blind,
And defined by the outcome.

—Divya Khanna

Contents

Foreword

The charm of this book is Divya's ability to keep the reader engaged in multiple narratives, simultaneously. From her personal experience, other stories and anecdotes and the insights she gleans from observation, the varied perspectives she weaves into the structure of the book —both from domain experts and from specially commissioned research—make it an easy and engrossing read.

Whilst the centre stage of the book is the ecosystem of business, the stories are human stories of ambition, aspiration, hard work, accomplishment, anxiety and feelings that cover the entire canvas of elation and ennui. Above all, it is about an honest conversation with oneself that helps us choose the path we end up choosing.

The range of the corporate culture discussion is wide, with some very interesting observations on deeply ingrained concepts of hierarchy that determine expectations, behaviors, gender determinants, etc. There are several nuggets embedded in the book—I particularly liked the demystifying of 'jugaad' as 'the desperate creations of people who have an urgent need, but lack the resources to fulfill it'. There is a certain poignancy in this observation through which we see a new dimension to something we are constantly surrounded by. And that is another refreshing quality of the book – it takes what is familiar and positions it in a new context with keen observation and authenticity.

Not surprisingly, the discontinuity caused by COVID in the lives of people and corporations is discussed in several contexts of lifestyle choices, work and personal priorities and implications for the workplace of the future. The importance of physical and mental well-being in the way people relate, together with attempting to understand the corporate landscape, is well covered in Parts 2 and 3 of the book, as are the expert reflections in the final part.

I applaud Divya for the courage of her convictions and the audacity to make herself vulnerable in telling a story that is genuine and straight from the heart and head.

Vinita Bali
Strategy Advisor and Independent
Director on boards in India and overseas

Note on Research Design and Methodology

Quantum Consumer Solutions did most of the qualitative research for this book, following the code of conduct laid down jointly by the Market Research Society of Great Britain and the Industrial Market Research Association of Great Britain.[1] Their study used a variety of research methodologies, which included individual depth interviews, paired interviews with working couples and gossip sessions between peers. It covered three consumer cohorts—freshers, middle managers and senior leaders of both genders, working across multinational corporations, Indian businesses and start-ups. The fieldwork covered Bombay and Delhi, with a pilot sample in Bangalore and was completed in October 2019.

Quantum Consumer Solutions[2] is one of the best market research agencies operating from India. Started by Dr Meena Kaushik in 1990, the agency has offices across India, Bangladesh, Sri Lanka, Indonesia, China, Singapore and London. Quantum

---

[1] The Market Research Society of India has not developed its own Code of Conduct

[2] https://www.quantumcs.com/

has a well-deserved reputation for their depth of insights and strategic inputs across consumers, categories and cultures. Anjana Pillai, Partner and India Board Member at Quantum Consumer Solutions, led this research project.

I have used a series of online surveys through SurveyMonkey, LinkedIn and Google Forms as well as several personal conversations with the experts and our combined network to supplement, validate and update the data and research insights for the last three years of the COVID-19 pandemic.

Online Surveys

1. Indian Corporate Culture (Lockdown Learning)—June 2020 on SurveyMonkey
2. Indian Corporate Culture #2 (Cultural Clash)—June–July 2020 on SurveyMonkey
3. Indian Corporate Culture #3 (Hierarchy Rules)—August 2020 on SurveyMonkey
4. How does Indian Corporate Culture Fare on Gender Equality and Sensitivity—August 2020 on LinkedIn Polls
5. The Need to Use Some Sort of Jugaad to get Work Done—September 2020 on LinkedIn Polls
6. The Biggest Attraction of a Corporate Career in India—January 2021 on LinkedIn Polls
7. What Best Defines a Bad Boss—March 2021 on LinkedIn Polls
8. Redefining Retirement—September 2021 on Google Forms
9. Redefining Retirement Follow-up—September 2021 on Google Forms
10. The COVID-19 Impact on our Work Culture—October–November 2021 on Google Forms

Panel of Experts Featured as Consultants and Contributors

Ashok Capoor is a business consultant and former president and managing director of Diageo-United Spirits Limited. With a background in sales and marketing, he is an acknowledged expert on the alcoholic beverage industry and also offers consultation services to private equity clients.

Kalyani Capoor is a mental health professional and cognitive therapist with over twenty years of experience in counselling private clients in Bombay and Bangalore. She was a guest columnist for *Savvy* magazine for two years. She conducts mental health workshops for corporate clients, having conducted several workshops for the Young Presidents' Organization (YPO) and Entrepreneurs' Organization (EO) forums.

R.R. Nair is an HR consultant, an independent director, coach for business leaders and former director-HR of Unilever group companies. He was selected for the National Award by the National Human Resource Department Network (NHRD) for his outstanding contribution to the HR profession in India. He was also conferred the Lifetime Achievement Award by the NHRD and by CNBC-KPMG. He contributed regularly to executive education efforts at the Indian School of Business (ISB), Hyderabad.

Rohit Krishan Gulati is an architect and design consultant with over twenty years of experience in workplace design. He is the principal architect at Incubis Architects and founder-director at Incubis Consultants (India) Pvt. Ltd., a multi-disciplinary design consultancy.

Introduction: A Crisis of Opportunity

Around five years ago, I was a typical textbook case of 'burnout'. I was a workaholic with no personal life; my health was unravelling, and I couldn't set aside enough time to take care of myself. I felt overworked and under-appreciated, losing both my motivation and my sense of purpose. I was beginning to doubt my ability. Had I hit my brick wall? Was it a hard stop to my career because I could no longer see the road ahead?

My health became the perfect excuse to take a break. A consultation with a financial planner made it a more comfortable decision. I felt so exhausted that I needed intensive physiotherapy and Ayurvedic treatment to get my health back into some sort of steadiness. As I took the time and effort to restore my health, I began to introspect on all the situations at work I had found tough and realized that much as I would have liked to cynically blame my burnout on a toxic corporate culture, it wasn't so simple.

Unlike some socio-religious cultures in India, the corporate culture does not have any rigidity and varies widely across industries and organizations. Yet, just as we tend to blame our political woes on 'the system', we tend to attribute our career lows to 'the culture'. We seem so certain of some unwritten rules of acceptable corporate behaviour that we accept them as rational explanations for our career trajectories. He refuses to work the weekend, so he will get overlooked for a promotion. She never leaves the office before her boss, so this must impress him into giving her a good increment. Coming to office even when I have a headache, or sending e-mails in the middle of the night show my commitment to the job. It's not done to refuse global conference calls at odd times to accommodate different time zones, especially when our counterparts there might be more vigilant about protecting their personal time. We are more hardworking, after all, and this is a source of pride for us Indians. Yet, hard work alone does not get us very far and can even be counterproductive as per my own experience.

Since there is no common rule book, corporate culture tends to be highly variable across companies, sectors and even functional departments. So, culture often becomes the excuse to change jobs or switch industries. We perceive start-ups as more casual, Indian businesses as more hierarchical and multinational corporations as more professional. Yet, we forget our own contribution and overlook our collective power.

'Culture does not make people. People make culture,' says Chimamanda Ngozi Adichie[1] in her book on feminism. Just as we can choose whether or not to perpetuate gender assumptions and stereotypes, we can also have some say in our workstyle and work environment. We seem to have forgotten this in our race to prove ourselves, win the approval of our bosses and impress our peers and community.

The burnout that happened to me seems to be a corporate rite of passage, but not everyone gives up or gives in to the pressure. Some have no choice but to stick with their career plans while some find ways to thrive in it.

---

[1] Chimamanda Ngozi Adichie, *We Should All Be Feminists*, (London: Fourth Estate, an imprint of Harper Collins Publishers, 2014).

I wanted to understand this better. Why did I feel trapped in my previous jobs despite the regular income, the good roles, the teams and resources at my disposal? I was successful in terms of the goals I had set at the beginning of my career, but I didn't feel successful. I felt that my achievements had come at too great a price. As I spoke to my trusted guides and mentors, I realized that I was re-evaluating and re-defining my ideas of success, in my career and in my life, and that the two were no longer as unconnected as they might have once seemed. As an ambitious young newbie with awkward social skills, I was more interested in proving my worth in a job than in building a life for myself. It felt reasonable then, but is it merely time and maturity that has influenced a change in my priorities, or was I wrong then or perhaps now?

As an account planner, I've always found it easier to uncover insights when I was looking in from the outside. I felt my break from the corporate world might help me finally understand what I couldn't when I was on the inside. I consulted experts in psychology, human resources, workspace design, marketing and business leadership and also contracted Quantum Consumer Solutions to do market research with me. We met people in different stages of their corporate careers in multinational companies, Indian businesses and start-ups across Bombay, Delhi and Bangalore.

The report was ready in February 2020 and my plan was to work on a book to share our collective insights. Then the COVID-19 pandemic reached India, and we have been in some form of lockdown since. Over three years later, it feels like life may never be quite the same again. Many from the corporate world are working from home but missing the office structure and camaraderie, some are reconnecting to simpler lifestyles while some are simply resentful of the endless video calls and relentless housework and childcare. Some people may be struggling with these issues, all at once. Many have ventured back to the office to find it both changed and strange. We are all challenged by the uncertainty.

The conversation I wanted to start through my book has already begun. This unanticipated situation has triggered mass re-evaluation of our work and life choices. In April 2020, we had wondered when our lives and careers would go back to the way they were, and by April 2021, we wondered if they would. Perhaps now, we should be wondering whether we want them to.

The post-COVID world is currently hard to imagine, given that there is no clear solution in sight. There is an opportunity in this crisis that we must not miss. Our companies, governments, investors, consumers, communities, families—all are braced for sudden changes. If we could use this momentum to re-design our work and personal lives, how would they look? How can we shape the Indian corporate culture to be more humane, engaging and productive? My aim with this book is to help us understand where we were and how we are evolving, to give us insights to reflect on so that we can make more deliberate and informed choices about where we can go from here.

Setting the Context: We Are What We Eat

The culture I was born into was dictated by chance. My family, religion and community determine clear dos and don'ts that were drummed into me from childhood. Even for regular home-cooked meals, it was mummy and papa who decided the menu and prescribed the minimum quantity that had to be eaten. I was only allowed a few quirks of my own. My dislike for onions was accepted and often there would be two versions of a family staple, one without onions for me and one with onions for the rest. The familiar childhood meal is always waiting for me at home, no matter how far I may travel from it. Similarly, my culture of birth is embedded in my life, lurking somewhere inside me, to which I return at will.

I find Indian corporate culture more like an extensive buffet spread—out of the ordinary, meant for a diverse group to share—trying to accommodate various palates and, often, overwhelming. Such sophistication is an acquired taste, and we want to get there quickly: to feel like we belong, to feel less out of place. We get to choose what we eat but we also want our choices to reflect well on us. Even if it means having to tolerate a few onions.

Viewed from the family dining table, the corporate spread represents aspiration in terms of status, material wealth and lifestyle—the upward mobility denied to us in our cultures of chance, the opportunity to exchange a fixed hierarchy for a progressive one and the lure of a world where we can shed some of our norms and taboos with legitimacy. Corporate designations can supersede caste and family roles. Every promotion can increase the family's social standing. Corporate socializing encourages sipping wine or whisky even if alcohol is not permissible at home. Young women and men can gain more independent lifestyles and postpone getting married and/or having children for the sake of their promising careers. It's the sort of excuse that can work well with our ambitious and competitive Indian families.

In our eagerness to belong to our culture of choice, we adopt behaviours that seem strange and uncomfortable, hoping that we will grow into them. We feel that our confidence will grow as we progress, and then we might even dare to change what we couldn't get used to. But initial conformation can become muscle memory; the knee-jerk responses are equally well programmed as our childhood dos and don'ts. The demands of the job can overwhelm our time and energy so that little is left for thinking things through.

R.R. Nair, leadership coach and former director-HR of Unilever group companies, talks of the dilemma faced by corporate freshers who are perhaps commanding an annual salary that surpasses the lifetime earnings of their parents. They have the dual burden of paying off their educational loans while maintaining a lifestyle in line with their corporate peers. 'Do we really know how to exercise our choices?' he asks, bringing up the story of the captive elephant. As a baby, the elephant can be secured to its post by a flimsy rope, but the same rope holds it prisoner as an adult when it can easily walk away. Everyone knows this but the elephant. It appears he chooses to remain captive but perhaps he doesn't feel like he has a choice.

It's easier to navigate the maze of corporate life if we just stick to the rules or know which ones are flexible. It takes a lot of confidence to build up the courage to be genuinely different. Rebelling in our birth culture is probably a little easier as it is somewhat cushioned by parental love. Corporate culture is more transactional, and the fear of ejection looms large. Not everyone is prepared to take the risks. What if our bluff is called? Are we prepared for the humiliation and rejection that might follow? Or is this just an imaginary fear of repercussions that may never come? We don't know for sure but we get a good sense of how this skews from the peer pressure in the office, which can be just as hard for us to resist as it is for teenagers in college. We don't outgrow our need to feel accepted, admired and be popular in the cultures we want to belong to. And let's not forget that success in the corporate world makes us look good back at home too.

Our corporate culture evolves from the choices we make, and keep on making, as we grow and mature in our careers and lives. None of them are set in stone, and we have the power to make, unmake or remake them, at any point. But do we have the bandwidth and time to make informed choices?

The results[1] of a survey I conducted via SurveyMonkey and LinkedIn in June 2020 suggest, we do not. 'Time to reflect' is one of the most-mentioned benefits of working from home that would be missed on returning to the office. In our hyper-busy lives, pre-COVID, we rarely had time to think, juggling work and family, managing homes and commutes. The pandemic has forced us out of our rigid routines into an unprecedented

---

1 Divya Khanna, 'A Crisis of Opportunity', LinkedIn, 2 June 2020. Available at https://www.linkedin.com/pulse/crisis-opportunity-divya-khanna/?trackingId=%2BmCfilRuRniujTGMTDfcvA%3D%3D

situation, where few days are alike, and we are forced to constantly reflect, evaluate and prioritize what we are doing, how, when and why.

I hope to fill our information gap with the insights from my research project. The respondents are from three distinct cohorts of age, experience and life stage, and I will share their experiences and choices in this book to help us review the full extent of the buffet spread that is available to us.

Each of us can decide what we put on our individual plates. And what we choose to eat.

PART 1
CULTURAL UNDERCURRENTS

1

The Corporate Caste System

'There should be a proper hierarchy level.' This is one of the first things said by Rohan, a mid-level IT consultant with clients around the globe, when we met at his house in Delhi. He feels that delegation of tasks is important so that managers can be free to make decisions, clearly drawing a boundary between the decision-makers and executors in an organization. It seems incongruous coming from him because his own organization is relatively flat, and he only has an occasional freelance technician to direct. He misses a hierarchical structure.

An organizational hierarchy is a solid form we can cling to in the midst of business challenges, with our roles and responsibilities clearly defined. It is practical to have the boundaries identified. However, this research project reveals that the inherent value of hierarchy in India is beyond such rational concerns.

Status-consciousness is one of the most conspicuous Indian traits. When we start a conversation for the first time, the introduction covers a variety of inquiries that help us size up the situation and define the boundaries of the engagement. We feel an urgent need to know where we stand in relation to the other person. Respect and deference need to flow the right way for us to be comfortable and for the conversation to go smoothly. It used to be predominantly community, caste, gender and age that dictated who deferred to whom. Such calculations were necessary to avoid giving offence, a social crime that could, and does in some parts of the country, lead to horrific consequences.

Today's boundaries are different in most parts of urban affluent India, where many people have corporate jobs. These are defined not so much by fixed notions of caste and community but by fluid concepts of designations and prospects, determined by qualifications and the pedigree of the institutes that provide them. Accountants versus engineers, an engineer from an Indian Institute of Technology (IIT) versus another perhaps equally good but less famous institute, an IIT engineer who also studied at an Indian Institute of Management (IIM) versus an IIT engineer who studied at another less lauded management education institution, an IIT–IIM Chief Executive Officer (CEO) of a multinational company versus an IIT–IIM CEO of an Indian business house, the present CEO versus his retired predecessor—the permutations are infinite, especially since age, gender, community and personal affiliations still play a role.

Saloni, an extroverted and focused young woman living in Delhi, works for an Indian start-up and enjoys the designation of 'growth manager'. She is only two years into her first job and appreciates the respect the tag of 'manager' brings her. It gives her an edge over the small business owners she interacts with for work. Her family and neighbourhood aunties and uncles are also suitably impressed. She feels proud of her accomplishments but acknowledges that it is her designation that is the real signal of her success.

The fluidity of a corporate career is like a game of snakes and ladders. There are opportunities for growth as well as risks of sliding down, played out against the backdrop of immense competition. Indian ambition and competitiveness are at the extreme end of the global spectrum. It starts young, with mothers competing over their babies' milestones and their children's school report cards and extracurricular activities. As we grow, we are used to being compared unfavourably, not just with our siblings and peers but also with older relatives and fictional characters from movies and TV serials. And while the competition may be tough over physical attributes we can or can't control, maximum intensity is reserved for our career prospects. Some parents try to direct this by enrolling children as young as six years into coaching classes for IIT-entrance exams or software coding. No wonder we live on tenterhooks and grow up to believe that one wrong step or one right step could break or make our careers.

Moving up the hierarchy is a constant endeavour and with every rung of the ladder that is conquered, there is immense pride. Karan, a general manager in an Indian company in Bombay, shares that he worked far harder to excel in his company's fast track programme than he did for his management education—'That is the reason that I am right now handling a national role because otherwise generally at my age people would not have reached there.'

Salaries and pride increase with every step up the ladder. So do status and the professional and social perks that come with an improved status. Rohit Krishan Gulati, an architect and design consultant with over twenty years of experience in workplace design, endorses this view. 'Majority of corporates in India are quite hierarchical as against an American organization where hierarchy doesn't play such a strong role in workplace design. In India, your aspiration is that when I go from junior management to senior management, I'll at least get a cubicle. When I move into senior management, I'll probably get a semi-private office, with people coming to meet me in my office rather than me going to the meeting room. This cultural mindset has never gone out of play in India, where the office structure and your office seat is also a marker of your position in the hierarchy. Whereas in an MNC or progressive Indian organization, where you sit is not necessarily a marker of your position.'

When I was a management trainee with a big advertising agency in Mumbai, I had to struggle to get my work done through the production studio. I was at the bottom of the corporate food chain—a trainee and a young woman, and I didn't speak Marathi, the primary language of most of the studio employees. I was the perfect target for bullying and an outlet for the frustration they couldn't express to anyone higher up the ladder. Two promotions later, on moving from an open workspace to a shared cubicle, all it took was a phone call or email and my work would stream seamlessly through the same studio. It used to constantly surprise me. I was still relatively young, still a woman, and I still couldn't speak Marathi—the only difference was, I had climbed the first two rungs of the ladder, and this changed the way the studio employees behaved with me. Instead of begging and pleading, I could now demand. This change in attitude and behaviour is a heady rush, and even on its own, a strong motivation for further progress.

Elevated status in professional and social circles means a change in most of our personal equations as well. Our deeply hierarchical society gives some leeway to corporate progress. Saloni (the growth manager, mentioned earlier) is a good example. As a daughter, she is expected to help her mother with household work, but her elevated designation and corporate success has translated into her mother treating her on par with her brother and not expecting any such help, except when she herself is unwell.

Climbing up the corporate ladder gives us the opportunity to overcome some of the inequalities in our society. The corporate designation becomes our primary identity and calling card, eliciting the respect and privileges we could not otherwise command. The higher the designation, the more powerful is the projection. We savour this hard-earned power just as much as we suffered from our powerlessness at the lower rungs, thus perpetuating the inequality of the corporate hierarchy.

The research report by Quantum Consumer Solutions points out, 'Employees at the lowest level are expected to handle menial tasks at the workplace (fetching tea, organizing schedules, doing manual paperwork) before they can climb up to a higher level where one is no longer required to take on such tasks. Additionally, this hierarchy also fosters an inherent disregard for employees at the lower levels as they hold very little power.'

With every rung we climb, we get more responsibility and more power, but how we handle that power can vary. Kalyani Capoor, practicing psychotherapist for over twenty years, who also conducts mental health workshops for corporate set-ups, notes, 'The more secure the primary identity and the higher the self-esteem, the less the individual needs to cling to, flaunt and project his/her corporate power. When a boss comes across as insensitive, reactive or aggressive, he/she is, more often than not, struggling with internal feelings of inadequacy. The more empowered you feel within, the less likely you are to misuse external power.'

Everyone I have spoken to has multiple anecdotes of a boss or client indulging in a power play, whether deliberate or unconscious—from insisting on bizarre meeting times or venues that suit their own convenience to outright public humiliation when work is not up to their expectations. It's interesting that such stories are always told from the perspective of the lower-ranked victim. Few leaders feel secure enough to tell these stories from their vantage point.

This reminds me of the practice of 'ragging' in some Indian colleges, where senior students tease the 'freshers' as an informal induction. This ranges from innocent pranks for the most part to some amount of progressively embarrassing tasks and even a few isolated cases of horrendous abuse. Freshers dread this rite of passage and usually feel humiliated when they go through it but when they become the seniors, their perspective changes. They feel entitled to inflict ragging on the latest batch of freshers, having gone through it themselves and also rationalizing that they are so much 'nicer' to their juniors than their seniors were to them.

If we can be honest with ourselves, we know that we all have, at some point, blown off steam at someone of lower status than ourselves because we know they can't retaliate. In my days as a management trainee, taxi drivers and my building security guard had become convenient outlets for my stress, just as I was for the production studio executives. I had believed that I was entitled to vent in this manner, and it is possible that the studio executives had believed the same. The deep inequalities of Indian culture inevitably seep into the corporate culture as well. As a friend once told me, 'Stress always flows downwards.'

Ashok Capoor, business consultant and former managing director of Diageo-USL, observes, 'There is a distinction in how most people behave towards their juniors and seniors at work. Juniors are treated more aggressively while seniors are flattered and pandered to.' If there was free-flowing interaction between the levels, this would be easier to notice. There is some contrast in how a person is perceived at work, depending on whether the perspective is from that of his boss or that of his subordinates.

Respondents to my survey on LinkedIn[1] from June–July 2020 claim 'respect for authority' as a shared value between Indian culture and corporate culture. They also mention two seemingly contradictory values as clashing between the two cultures. The first is 'speaking up' to authority figures in a corporate setting and the second is 'not rocking the boat' by careful avoidance of controversial discussions. This points towards the supremacy of the boss in the Indian office. While it's important to have an opinion and state it, it's also critical to toe the line between giving information and giving offence. The boss commands substantial respect, ranging anywhere from subtle deference to outright subservience. 'There is a thin but very distinct line between respect for authority and fear of authority. Respect for authority and clear structure is a healthy prerequisite for any unit to function effectively, be it family or organization. Respect for authority allows rational questioning and encourages independent thinking; fear of authority does not! An authoritarian environment fosters fear rather than respect. It's not just respect but fear of authority that props up the status hierarchy, whether in the corporate context or the social context,' says Kalyani Capoor.

'Managing the boss' is a critical aspect of our careers, and we believe that it largely determines whether we are headed for the ladders or the snakes. This is not to say that egalitarian leaders do not exist in India. Ashok Capoor distrusts 'yes-men'. He says, 'You need to empower your direct reports to foster creativity and innovation, which comes from challenge and dissent. If they are only saying yes to whatever you suggest, you are not doing your job as a leader.' I have heard several anecdotes of empowering leaders, though just not as many as

---

1 Survey results available at https://www.linkedin.com/pulse/survey-results-we-what-eat-divya-khanna/?trackingId=8xYSqsPwSm9arn2yn8p%2FGg%3D%3D

those of the domineering leaders. Perhaps it makes for better storytelling, or perhaps there are just too few of them around.

HR expert, R.R. Nair[2] has observed a clash as the culture shifts. 'Perceived notions about how a boss should behave is scripted early in life as a result of multiple interactions with authority figures. Hierarchy is not going anywhere soon but the younger generation is pushing for a softer hierarchy where some questioning and challenging of the powers is accepted. This is especially challenging for leaders who are used to working in a command and control mode and demand unquestioning loyalty and compliance from their subordinates.'

The demand for more equality and flatter corporate structures are noted in the Quantum report but the need for a clear hierarchy dominates. 'Today, many corporates are grappling with the idea of balancing both; however, in a culture that is deeply hierarchical, employees still seek guidance on role clarity in order to structure relationships and assign individual responsibilities and set expectations from people at various levels.' Any ambiguity tends to lead to confusion and territorial squabbling.

I expected, as many probably did, that the extended periods of remote working during the many lockdowns might have diluted the corporate hierarchy but the results of my survey on Google Forms from September–October 2021 show otherwise. 'The hierarchy is that much more apparent and experienced as one cannot connect at an individual level given the limited face time,' says Jaya, a senior-level manager who works from home in Bombay. Most respondents acknowledge and appreciate the changes in the attitudes and actions of top management in terms of increased empathy, developing

[2] CEO coach for business leaders and former director-HR of Unilever group companies

support systems and more frequent check-ins through technology interfaces but they also view these as contextual reactions to the pandemic and temporary measures that are oriented towards achieving business outcomes. Chaitanya, from Bangalore, says, 'Everyone including senior management is affected by COVID. There is definitely a shift in attitude, but how long that will last is the question.'

Corporate hierarchy in India is stronger because of the cultural bias towards hierarchy in Indian society. It is not just the caste system but also the community and family structures as well as the colonial heritage that drive this. We are used to being told what our place is, deferring to those above us and in turn, expecting deference from those below us. The corporate hierarchy is different from other hierarchies in the fact that we can move up and down in it more easily. With every step up or down, the social rules change. And this impacts our own behaviour and that of the people around us. So, while we may protest and rebel against the other hierarchies, we protect and preserve this one. This hierarchy is in our favour, provided we can climb all the ladders and avoid all the snakes.

2

Working in a Pressure Cooker

The first time I cooked dal is an amusing memory. I had slaved over it for hours in my family's tiny kitchen in midtown Manhattan, but it didn't look anything like the picture in the recipe. I called my sister to take a look, and we took turns using a large wooden spoon to mash the dal into submission. It became somewhat edible but when a guest ventured a tentative compliment, I confided in her how long it had taken to cook. She asked, 'How many whistles did you allow it to cook for in the pressure cooker?'

My sister and I were surprised that it hadn't even occurred to us to use a pressure cooker, the staple of most Indian kitchens. It traps the increasingly hot air inside to allow the food to be cooked with an intensity that shortens the time required. Experienced cooks measure the food's readiness by the number of its periodic whistles, which release the excess steam. It works quite well unless you are a novice who forgets to monitor the whistles, in which case you may be left with an inedible mess.

I feel the pressure cooker is an apt analogy for the competitive business environment in India. We keep increasing the pressure to reduce the time taken to do the work so we can get more work done. The pressure takes many forms—from audacious, near-impossible targets to stretching our physical and mental limits. The most common theme is the 'commitment demonstration', where we feel compelled to show that work is our number one priority.

Sonia and Kabir, a newly wed couple, live in Bangalore. Kabir works in sales for an up-and-coming start-up while Sonia is in transition mode. She has recently given up her hectic design job for an HR role in the expectation of starting a family. The first year of their marriage was an adjustment, complicated by the demands of their jobs. Kabir had been so busy chasing his promotion that they barely had any time together. 'It is very normal for us to be summoned for midnight meetings which get termed as pizza parties. We don't get to say no to this.' He is vague about the consequences of skipping a midnight meeting and yet, he clearly doesn't want to be the one to find out. Both believe this sacrifice of the personal for the professional is necessary to secure their family's future.

Quantum Consumer Solutions' research report observes, 'The idea of training oneself to focus all of one's energy on the goal, by going through a process of extreme rigor makes one compromise on aspects such as sleep, socialization, self-care etc. This leads to an acceptance and normalization of practices such as working overtime/late hours, taking on too much work, compromising on time for family/self, etc., especially during the early years in one's career.'

We noticed a theme in the gossip sessions shared by our own circles of friends and peers—a contest of sorts in comparing the pressures each is facing. Who gets by on less sleep, who works on more weekends, who is more stressed—these are the new war stories that grant us bragging rights. We may not be doctors saving lives or soldiers at the frontline risking our own lives, but we believe we can and should be just as dedicated and self-sacrificing.

Manu, a twenty-eight-year-old operations manager in the Delhi–NCR area, shares how his relationship became a casualty of his job commitment when he chose to skip his girlfriend's birthday party to attend to an emergency situation at work. He thought she would understand, but she broke off the relationship. During the gossip session with his best friends, Manu claims to have made the right call but his morose body language and the way he repeatedly refers to the girl in question as 'my beloved' tells a different story. He is still struggling with the heartbreak.

As a young management trainee, barely two months into the job, I found myself in a situation where the entire team was suddenly vacant. The team of a dozen people was reduced to only the vice president, who led the team, and me. I was out of my depth. I expected my job list to adjust to this reality, but it only got longer. I expected some leeway and guidance from the VP, but he only turned up the pressure. Somehow, I survived this period, extremely shaken but also slightly more competent. 'Trial by fire' is how the VP described it to a confidante of mine when questioned why he threw me into the deep end instead of immediately filling the vacancies. I can't help but wonder if there could have been another way—if I would have performed better if I had time to learn and if every item on my job list did not come with a 'do or die' undercurrent to it.

Ashok Capoor believes that the pressure needs to be set just right. 'Pressure can play a positive role when the environment in the organization is non-threatening. After empowering your team, you need to have complete trust on their capability to deliver. This always works wonders and people put their hearts and souls to give their best. Only if they fail to deliver, then you can probably check out where they went wrong and how it can be corrected in the future.'

No pressure, and there is a lethargy that develops. Too much pressure, and burnout looms. Just the right pressure and you get results. As any good cook will tell you, getting the pressure just right is an art and one that requires your complete attention and readiness to keep adjusting it. When each person is focused on dealing with the pressure on them rather than monitoring the pressure that they pass along, the intensity can get out of control.

I mentioned the downward flow of stress in the previous chapter on hierarchy. We are culturally conditioned to communicate less assertively with our seniors and more aggressively with our juniors. The result is a hesitation to push back on the pressures we face from the top and a tendency to pass along all that we can't handle downwards. The board of directors may have given the CEO some hard targets that he feels he can neither justify nor oppose. The best way he knows to handle this is to pass them along to his senior management team, breaking the targets into functional goals and encouraging the internal competition between them. Each of them, determined to prove their individual worth, will take on the audacious goals and share them down the line to their teams. The pressure gets passed through the system to the frontline employees, extending to vendors, suppliers, service providers, even to the administrative staff, who will face the brunt of tempers snapping when the whistles blow with overwhelming steam.

This example only tracks the external pressure flowing through the corporate hierarchy. In reality, this pressure tends to collide and collude with internal pressures that come from a highly competitive, status-driven society and an individual's own pressure to prove their worthiness and provide well for their families.

'Given our cultural conditioning, our work and self-worth are almost seamlessly fused. Any criticism or questioning of our work output, very often, is experienced as a threat to our self-worth. This threat perception leads to anxiety and self-doubt. The external pressure of work demands and deadlines is now further compounded by this internal pressure,' says Kalyani Capoor. 'Our personal and professional are rarely, if ever, air-tight compartments. Personal unresolved issues intrude at work and stress that builds up at work often explodes at home.'

This complicates leaders' efforts to monitor the pressure, given that some of their employees may respond well while others may break down at the same level. Few leaders would have the bandwidth to fine-tune to this extent, given that they are also focused on facing their own pressures.

Minaxi Indra, business leader and president, UpGrad for Business, is familiar with the complexity of managing large teams. She observes, 'Team members align with the organizational goals and sales targets better when they understand "how" their individual quota impacts the business' profitability and revenues. It is important that business heads ensure that quotas are reflective of the organizational priorities, the macroeconomic reality and the tenure/experience of the salesperson. A failure to manage this trifecta results in employee burnout and unproductive pressure on the team. In order to get the best performance from employees, it is critical to understand the internal motivators of team members. In my experience, I've seen team members supersede their own expectations when they find their internal aspirations aligned with the business goals expected from them and a business leader who has their back.'

It is difficult to reveal the full extent of the pressures we face at work and even more so, what we face in our personal lives. Not all leaders are aware, some may not be actively engaged and many more would just not have the time. More importantly, we believe that we must not complain about the sacrifices we make. Denying ourselves the right to vent about the pressures that truly weigh down on us, our only outlet is the superficial problems that everyone faces and sees in the same light.

Respondents in the research were eager to vent about the infrastructural issues that come with living in Indian cities. The commute time, traffic and state of the roads were top-of-mind complaints though the difficulty of school admissions, general inefficiency and corruption were also mentioned. There was a discernible pattern in the city-specific complaints—from Bangalore's poor road situation and unpredictable traffic and Mumbai's disruption due to metro-construction work to the residents of Delhi–NCR losing time in commuting across states. It is additional time taken away from the individual and is highly resented because this adds to the pressures of performing at work and giving time to the family. The commute may be the only time one may have for oneself, but it comes with its own guilt and pressure. Many try to work through it by replying to emails, catching up on reading and making calls. No one pauses to consider that perhaps 'the rush hour traffic' might not exist if office locations and timings were not so closely aligned across organizations of all types and sizes.

The COVID crisis is one more pressure amongst many others already layered on too thick. There has been a lot of discussion through articles, podcasts and webinars on how work can or should be managed now. Many leaders and companies are grappling with working in this situation, but I find their emphasis is on delivering more, not less, with greater efficiency expected and managers doing a lot more direct monitoring. This appears to be an experiment to turn up the heat and see what happens rather than slow down and reorganize expectations, much like what I experienced as a management trainee.

Most of the respondents to my survey on Google Forms from September–October 2021 feel an increased sense of pressure at work. Anshu, from Hyderabad, who is working partly from home and partly from office, says, 'The work pressure is high and it's become relentless. It's blurred the lines between work and personal time and is increasingly eating into the work-life balance.' As mentioned in the earlier chapter, respondents appreciate the increased empathy due to the pandemic but feel that the focus remains on achieving business results. They believe that there is additional pressure to perform due to the flexibility and technology that is now provided to them. Many have pointed out a significant disadvantage of flexible or remote working. 'You have very little control on your time as you are expected to be available anytime,' says Dilip, a senior-level manager in Bombay. Maya, who has a similar profile, says, 'There is no wasting time in traffic. However, longer working hours have offset that. Ironically, work has gone up, both at home and at work.'

Technology and the lack of commuting are creating more time but instead of using this extra time for ourselves or our families, we are looking for ways to use it to do more work. The Quantum research report points out that 'Hard work and strenuous effort is culturally considered the key to success. The emerging demand for smart and efficient work currently works against the idea of hard work. Hard work gives one the recognition of being a dedicated employee and reassures one that they are on the path to success. However, smart work allows efficient use of time and resources, and even though it is not culturally recognized, it is in alignment with the corporate need for efficiency and maximization of time. More people are being pushed to pursue the idea of smart work, which most are not culturally attuned to. There is still considerable glorification of hard work that happens in Indian corporates. And there is some discomfort with the fact that smart work could be seen as a lazy/quick fix effort.'

Kabir (from the couple mentioned earlier) understands that the projection is as important as the reality. He says, 'Money will come anyway, what you don't get easily is growth. You have to show that you are working hard even if you are not meeting your targets.' If the targets are near impossible to achieve or unrealistic in the current business context, then showcasing hard work is all that's left to deal with the anxiety of job layoffs. People working from home across industries mention excessive Zoom calls and webinars as bosses feel the need to constantly check on their employees who, in turn, feel the need to justify their roles.

I had a moment of clarity five years ago when a cousin and I were swapping war stories about the strain we were feeling from our jobs. He said, 'I am an investment banker so I get a lot of money for doing this. What are you doing it for?' It gave me pause. I was not making a lot of money, I was missing my sleep, and compromising my health and the few precious relationships I had. What was I trying to prove to myself or anyone else? I find I still have the need to push myself to do my best, to prove that I'm worthy. It's not bad in general, but every once in a while, it turns into an obsession that leaves me anxious, irritable and exhausted.

R.R. Nair reflects on the early phase of his own career journey involving long spells of residential courses that he had to direct as well as frequent travel and relocations with a hint of regret, 'My self-imposed standards of excellence drove me to continuously reinvent, renew and revitalize myself to face life's challenges. In retrospect, one of the unintended consequences has been that I did not find enough time at home. I believe there is a lesson for all of us; kids must have first right for your time.' Kalyani Capoor agrees, 'Genuine personal relationships offer good immunity against stressors at work. Ironically corporate demands often leave very little or no time to invest or engage in them.'

Ritu, a senior manager at a global technology company, believes in setting her boundaries at work. She says, 'In today's workplace scenario of "working at home", I feel the pressure to be available twenty-four hours a day. Creating some clear boundaries is helping me reduce work-life conflict and the stress that goes with it, especially in these difficult times. For me that has been making a rule to take some time for physical activity, not checking emails from late evening and not answering the phone during dinner. While my role in a support function makes this a little easier to implement, sometimes it's still a challenge since people expect you to be available if there is urgency.'

Job function plays a role in how much we feel we can push back. Many people in sales and other client-facing roles feel it would be career suicide to not always be available on the phone, if not on email. Like Sonia (from the couple I mentioned earlier), many women feel the need to step back from more demanding work roles when they anticipate greater demands on their time from family.

Indian history glorifies sacrifice. Our heroes are people who fought against tremendous odds to achieve goals that seemed impossible. Mahatma Gandhi is a good example. His challenges were complex, his personal sacrifices many and what he achieved was once unimaginable. As we seek the materialistic success of the corporate world in a liberal economy, the beliefs we carry about how to achieve success remain rooted in the past. We still attach status and accomplishment to the most hard-working person. Every success story reported in the news or reimagined into a movie contrasts the difficulties of the obstacles and the size of the personal sacrifices with the audaciousness of the victory. We tend to fit our personal narratives to a similar trajectory, feeling the need to justify our successes and rationalize our failures, accepting the intensifying pressure as a necessary condition for success.

3

Gender Guides

Raat din ka farak (the difference between night and day) is a popular Hindi idiom that corresponds to comparing apples and oranges. This is the constant justification for differences in the way in which gender is perceived, programmed and perpetuated in our country. Parents use it when their daughters complain about their limited freedom and their sons complain about being constantly sent on errands. Society uses it when women and men step too far out of their designated spaces. Organizations use it for making decisions on salaries, promotions and layoffs.

We cannot switch gender off.

In the broader social context, women of all strata and their families have safety concerns top of mind, and this remains the unspoken undercurrent behind every decision. Patriarchy in the urban affluent space, where most of corporate India resides, is unlike the rude crude aggression of certain rural communities where arbitrary male councils can prescribe whether women should wear jeans or use mobile phones and where fathers, brothers and husbands get murderous in the name of honour. Chivalry in the Indian context is about being protective. It comes from a benevolent and protective intent, which makes it that much harder to overcome its condescension and patronage.

My father always encourages me to not limit my ambitions due to gender stereotypes, but his protectiveness dilutes his intent of empowerment. Our corporate culture is similar in attitude. While its intent is to remove the obstacles women face and protect their safety, it ends up imposing limitations on their progress by reinforcing society's biases.

There are four spirited women in our last gossip session in Delhi. Devika, Prerna, Stuti and Meera are between twenty-four and twenty-six years of age and have been best friends since they first met in college. Stuti's family is more conservative than the others', and the friends had to combine forces to convince Stuti's mother to let her work. They are each other's support systems and confidantes. Devika claims she doesn't want to get married as it involves 'too many responsibilities', and she doesn't want to share her salary. The other girls don't appear to take her very seriously, all claiming that they will be married in three to five years. 'There is no pressure of marriage; we are focusing on our work now,' says Meera. The difficulties of managing both career and family are too far away to concern them now. They acknowledge that their families prefer them to have corporate careers because of the facilities provided for women's safety and commute. 'Dad knows everything; we have a GPS system and can also complain to and mail our senior and manager. We have guards who carry guns,' says Prerna.

Cheryl is a vibrant and impressive woman in her thirties. She started her career in the travel industry, spent a little time in real estate and now heads a big sales team for an international company in interior design. Her job is challenging, and she clearly enjoys it. She loves to travel and meet people, has never once failed in exceeding her sales targets and is proud of the career she has built for herself. Her husband is a doctor at a corporate hospital and prefers a more balanced life but supports all her ambitions. Despite her high self-confidence and feeling admired and valued within the organization, Cheryl seems all too aware of her limitations, 'If I get pregnant and suddenly I change the job, what if I am not able to handle everything. So being a female I guess that you have to think about those things, because the company doesn't understand. Not every company understands. If your job is sales oriented and if you are not giving business to the company, then I feel you have zero value over there.'

'It is a commonly found pattern that women seriously contemplate leaving their jobs/moving to a less challenging profile post marriage. The chances of a woman doing so is observed to be significantly higher post childbirth,' says the research report by Quantum Consumer Solutions. There are some companies that are trying to accommodate and leverage this potential workforce through new business models and innovative policies, but they often end up emphasizing the gender difference, with perceptions of 'women-friendly' often being equated to 'women-only'. Ashok Capoor says, 'It is heartening to note that more women are being included in the workforce and that HR policies are being made to accommodate their needs and create practical solutions. However, in many corporations, there is more lip service than actual changes in attitude.'

Women's issues are at the forefront of gender conversations at work primarily because gender diversity is becoming a priority for most senior management teams, demanded by some stakeholders and mandated by government requirements. 'Companies are driven by their business continuity requirement,' says R.R. Nair. 'The change in gender diversity in higher education institutes, especially the non-IIT technical institutes, where women make up 30–40 per cent of the student base, has been noted. Companies want to capitalize on this talent pool. At the same time, there is a challenge for the employer brand to be perceived as one that provides a fair and equitable work environment for everyone.'

The attempts to correct the gender imbalance are bringing up some issues for men, which if left unaddressed, might end up widening the gender gap. Quantum's research report highlights the challenge of getting both genders on the same page within a highly competitive context: 'Many women feel that their role at the workplace is not as significant as the ones assigned to their male counterparts. They are also subjected to unequal pay and unfair treatment by their own managers. But most women feel the need to passively fight the unfairness by continuing to work hard and prove themselves, so as to get an equal opportunity. Men, on the other hand, feel that women are provided unfair privileges—permission to leave early from work, more tolerance towards mistakes, long maternity leaves, choice of not working after pregnancy etc. These deep-seated patriarchal views foster a negative culture and hostile emotion towards women at the workplace.'

Women and men are pitted against each other at the workplace but in most homes, they are a team. Though many would say that gender roles are more pronounced in the context of the family, we observe that husbands and wives generally work together to get their own sense of balance, to negotiate their careers and lives, keeping in mind what will work in the best interests of their family.

Sonali is a legal manager in Mumbai. She and Ravi have a child, whose first birthday was coming up when we met at their family home in Bombay. Ravi's current position in a Japanese company is a promotion that he earned by taking up an offsite assignment during Sonali's pregnancy. He seems to resent his sacrifice while Sonali doesn't appear to blame him. 'I don't want extra money, I want extra time,' he says, as he describes how his current boss insists that he goes to work on Saturdays. 'I say I'll do the work, but I won't come to the office on Saturdays. It's affecting my relationship with the boss, but I'm very clear—first family, then money.'

Preeti and Varun, an older couple with a fifteen-year-old son, are both comfortable in the prime of their careers. They went through a tough phase when their son was unwell for two years. Both parents cut back on work and relied on the support of bosses and colleagues, but Preeti bore most of the brunt. 'It played in my psyche from seeing my parents work, my mother at her teacher's job and my father at his government job, that work is important and that I also have to be available to my child all the time,' she says. While both have had very demanding jobs in the past, currently Preeti's role as project manager in a multinational company is more challenging than Varun's job in finance in an Indian company. 'She made more sacrifices earlier in our careers, so now I accommodate. We are work-life partners. This can't work if one person is the priority all the time,' Varun says, describing his flexible working hours.

There are some advantages to the patriarchal perspective but only when women and men conform to the stereotype. Ambitious men who put their career first and nurturing women who put their family first have some advantage. But they are also open for exploitation. The former can be made to work almost round the clock with the promise of a promotion or increment, while the latter can be made to compromise on remuneration and designation in return for the flexibility provided. If a woman is ambitious, she can be treated like her male counterpart but with lesser-value promises and can also be an advertisement of the company's progressiveness. If a man wants more time with his family, he can be given that flexibility in exchange for lesser remuneration, and sometimes he may also become an object of ridicule for his colleagues.

I have not held a full-time job for a few years now. While I feel some pressure to reconfigure my path, I know that it is nowhere close to what I would face if I were a man. As a woman, I have the luxury of choosing not to work outside of the home and, even, not earning at all. My personal reservations aside, there would be little social judgement were I to decide that I'm okay relying on my father or a hypothetical spouse for financial support. Were a man to make such a choice, our society would be much more judgemental.

There are couples among who the wife holds the steady job and brings in the salary, while the husband pursues a creative and/or entrepreneurial passion. Whatever the understanding between the couple, often the joint projection to family and society is that this is a temporary phase. The husband will either succeed or give up after a period of time, returning to his role as the family's provider. In some circles, the switchover of gender roles is even celebrated but it may be a long time before this perspective is allowed entry into the cultural mainstream.

Tanya, a senior sales professional, was recently laid off. She and her husband decided to reorganize their finances given the current situation of the job market. Part of their plan was to approach the owner of their rented apartment in Bandra to request a reduction in rent. Even though the lease is in Tanya's name, their landlord, a retired professional from a leading Indian company, refused to consider any reduction in rent. He insisted that they could afford the rent because her husband must be the family's primary breadwinner. Tanya feels sure that had her husband been the one to lose his job, they might have got a more sympathetic response. She also suspects her former employer of a similar bias given that the three women from her team were all laid off while all the men retained their jobs.

The pandemic situation has, by force, altered the gender equation at home and given men sudden visibility into the details of household work and all that it takes. By taking on some of the chores like washing dishes and cleaning, they have a clearer understanding of the sheer repetitiveness and monotony of these tasks and the effort, time and energy these require. My survey on Google Forms from September–October 2021 shows that the gender gap at home has narrowed for nearly every respondent though the changes seem enduring only for those who already had more progressive views. Chaitanya, from Bangalore, says, 'Personally the respect for women, regardless of whether they are working or non-working, has increased way more. Gender gaps definitely have decreased, but a lot more is required.'

While men are helping more, women consider themselves responsible for taking care of household and do most of the work. There are many reasons for this, but mostly due to women themselves. From the better skills that women have developed through experience to their own rising standards of cleanliness, they seem to have lower tolerance for the inefficiency of novices and impatience with their learning curves. 'A woman at home is first perceived as a mom, then a working mom. And with family at home too, her constant juggle between home and work needs continues,' says Suma from Mumbai. She adds, 'Men just don't seem to be wired to obsess over home chores as a woman is. Besides, women have developed OCDs in COVID-19, and have had, those many added, cleanliness related jobs. Men, however, have shared responsibilities and have not been fussy about immaculate conditions, as they used to be earlier. They have cooked, cleaned, got involved in child and pet care etc.' It appears as if men face an invisible barrier preventing them from complete involvement with household responsibilities just as women do at work. None of the respondents felt there were any positive changes in the gender gap at work due to the pandemic.

'That women are held hostage to stereotypes is obvious and evident. One doesn't need to be particularly perceptive to see that. Being a woman, my understanding of the issue was instinctive, my empathy organic,' says Kalyani Capoor. 'It was my professional experience as a therapist with Indian men that sensitized me to the stereotypical expectations that they felt the pressure to live up to. Core beliefs like men should always be strong and in charge, men should always be the providers, men shouldn't be vulnerable or afraid ever, shouldn't ask for help, should earn such and such . . . are conditioned early and deep.'

I conducted a quick poll on LinkedIn in August 2020 to check personal perceptions of gender bias in Indian corporate culture. As you can see from the chart below, only seven people said they believed the corporate culture was fair to both genders.

How does Indian corporate culture fare on gender equality and sensitivity?

You can see how people vote. **Learn more**

Good – fair to both	17%
Ok but better for men	55%
Ok but better for women	7%
Bad – unfair to both	21%

42 votes • Poll closed

For too long, men's lives have been positioned as aspirational to women. Since they have the freedom that women want and have to fight for, it has been easy to ignore that they also face social pressures and biases and are vulnerable.

The #MeToo movement has, quite unintentionally, brought this to the surface. Women speaking out with broad-based public and media support have forced the corporate world to acknowledge the crimes against them, to redefine gender discrimination and to train their workforce better. Complaints from women employees can no longer be simply brushed aside to protect the organization's reputation and business. One side effect is that men are beginning to fear women too. They are now as anxious about being misinterpreted and unjustly accused, of being framed and victimized, as women have always been.

If senior men were earlier hesitant to mentor young women, they are now terrified. The perceived role-reversal of victims and villains has added more wariness. And now, that wariness is equally reciprocated on both sides. An ex-colleague once confided in me that she was more worried about her son than her daughter. Her daughter, she felt, was adequately trained to be cautious but her son was totally unprepared. She needed to teach him the wariness for the opposite sex that she had already instilled in her daughter. As women, we learn early on to calibrate our own behaviour and to steer clear of people and gestures that make us uncomfortable, irrespective of whether they have bad intent or not. Men have not been taught to behave so circumspectly.

'There is a certain neural comfort in categorizing. And research indicates that the human brain is predisposed to negative stereotyping,' says Kalyani Capoor. 'Any collective mind-set that polarizes people on criteria of gender, age, race etc. irrespective of which polarity it empathizes with, can't be healthy or functional.'

Everyday interactions between men and women are highly subjective and sensitive to interpretation. All women are trying to balance it out, learning to read between the lines and taking time to evaluate what they feel comfortable with. Sometimes, the gender biases work in their favour but mostly they do not. Women learn to jump through hoops to prove themselves. Now more men are realizing that they have also been trapped in the same situation though on the opposite side. They too must learn to balance, to read between the lines and find their own level of comfort. They must also have the opportunity to challenge the biases that hold them imprisoned. Men and women are continually learning to negotiate the biases of Indian society together as teams of spouses, friends, siblings or as a family. Can we also cooperate as colleagues to have each other's backs or will we always be competitors?

Among the respondents we meet, there is certain wistfulness for things to be different. Most of the women show an urgent ambition in the wake of their biological clocks' ticking. Most of the men show a brimming desire for more closeness with their families. Perhaps, it is a case of wanting more of what is scarce or of scoring points for not being the same as everyone else. Or maybe both men and women yearn for a balance, or to not be told what they can or cannot do. Both genders crave respect for being themselves rather than a stereotype and for answering to their feelings rather than society's dictates.

In an unequal world, all women are not victims, and all men are not villains nor does feminism aim to make it vice versa. Addressing issues related to women does not make issues related to men unimportant. True equality is when both men and women do not feel the pressure to choose between the binaries of villain or victim but instead exist in a similar space of opportunities and challenges. Women's labour deserves to be valued equally in monetary terms, and men need equal flexibility to attend to their families and for self-care. Can the corporate world become equally friendly to both genders and set the precedent for bringing night and day closer together?

4

The Personal and the Political

Saying that Indians are competitive is redundant. It's obvious in every sphere of life, from the sly shoving forward in queues everywhere to the reckless racing on the roads. Many of our brands have been built on getting one up on our neighbours and peers, whether in the whiteness of our shirts or the technology of our television sets. We have learned from early childhood that we must always strive to be first. And this mindset persists in the workplace where getting ahead of our peers is a priority.

I've already mentioned the similarity of our approach to our careers to a game of snakes and ladders in the earlier chapter on hierarchy. The ladders are visibly clear—the opportunity for increments, bonuses and promotions. The snakes are subtle. 'Office politics' is the misty haze where most people seem to stumble and which they hold responsible for any backsliding in position and prospects. Yet, it's always spoken of from the outside, as if it's a separate entity completely distinct from us and over which we have neither influence nor interaction of any kind.

Devika, an accounts executive with a global media company in Delhi, says, 'Those who are in high position make their group and they talk about us. And if you get success in less time, that is also something that people cannot digest.' She feels targeted by a clique of senior colleagues for her success and her rapport with her boss and team members. In the same session, her friend, Prerna, a financial analyst at a consulting firm, complains about partiality. 'The people the boss likes get leaves more easily. One manager has two [female employees] who are his favourite. If they make a mistake, he will take care of it and also gives leaves to them, and when we ask for leave, he does not give permission.' It's interesting to note that both friends sympathize with and support each other without noticing the incongruence in their situations and perspectives.

Mohit is at the start of his career with an upcoming Indian start-up in Bombay. He says, 'Undeserving people get promoted for [sucking up to the boss]. Some people are good at this, but I'm not. Deserving people don't get promoted and resign. My friend resigned from this company after working hard for three years. He had a good record at work but didn't get promoted.'

It's easy for Mohit to condemn people who can easily connect with their bosses because he is unable to do so, and it is just as easy for Devika to condemn those who would accuse her boss of favouritism. There is a parallel to this in the central conflict of the Indian epic the Mahabharata. Who should be the king of the Kuru clan? The Pandavas and Lord Krishna support the right of Yudhishthira as the eldest son of the previous king, Pandu. Their argument of primogeniture, the right of the eldest son to inherit, fails to acknowledge that Pandu was the younger son, made king ahead of his elder brother, Dhritarashtra. The Kauravas support Duryodhana, the eldest son of Dhritarashtra, the present king, and their argument fails to acknowledge that Yudhishthira's father was the king before Duryodhana's father. Each side is so intent on winning that they fail to see the weaknesses in their own logic and the strengths of the other side. Our personal perspective is just as firmly fixed when it comes to our careers and the context around them just as complex.

It's easy to disassociate and distrust people who are not like us, and it's equally easy to trust and connect with people who are more similar. Alumni networks, community or regional affiliations, gender and age cohorts—all of these help us identify the likeminded whom we can attempt to befriend. We need someone to have the occasional coffee or lunch with, to get the buzz around the office from, someone we can share with and who knows and gets where we are coming from. Sometimes, the suspicion of an external enemy can further strengthen these relationship bonds. The cliques that form in opposition to each other are both the cause of and the refuge from office politics. Shared perspectives reinforce and enable each other.

Shalini recently shifted with her husband to Chennai. He works in the finance industry, with a global bank, while her expertise is in marketing and advertising. Shalini's husband is Tamil and she's fluent in the language so she did not anticipate too much of an adjustment. She knew that the work environment would not be as cosmopolitan as she was used to. Yet, she is shocked by how judgemental her colleagues in a family-owned and managed fashion business are towards her. 'When I am thirty-seven years and don't have kids, it means I am selfish and too career-oriented. And therefore, I am a bad woman. If I dress well at work, it means I am not getting enough attention from my husband at home so here I am, trying to get the attention of other men,' she says.

Shalini feels targeted for her lifestyle choices because they do not conform to the traditional choices favoured by her colleagues. 'The senior management is from the family who owns the business and this is reflective of their attitudes,' she says. 'None of the Heads of Departments are women and none of them open their mouths. The employees down the line need the income and don't question the cultural mindset. The ones like me who speak up tend to be more privileged, so we have been branded the "rebellion maamis" at work.'

The Quantum research report points out, 'While active participation in politics is not required (neither do employees admit to this), it is important to be aware of the undercurrents, and stay on top of it so as to navigate potential threats when the time comes.'

Why are we so attuned to look for threats? Kalyani Capoor says, 'Having an evolutionary brain, we are hard-wired for threat perception. Survival still operates as a primal need and any perceived threat to that survival activates our neural alarm system. Like our animal ancestors, we compete to survive. The dangers are different; the jungle has changed but the competition hasn't.' The race to get ahead at work is just one more competition and we see the threats in our way in much the same way as our primitive brain would see an actual snake.

Our society is judgemental. It is generally culturally acceptable to comment on physical appearance, ask personal questions and even offer unsolicited advice. Single people are advised to get married or told what to do to be attractive to the opposite sex. Childless men and, especially, women are told to have babies. Overweight people are teased relentlessly. Finances are questioned and discussed openly. We know the drift. And it's useful when we need to navigate through the mists of office politics, to build our own counter narratives.

Innuendo, gossip and malicious branding are the tools of the insecure and the threatened, but this understanding is cold comfort when you are the target. I remember one incident early in my career, where I thought I was having an informal chat with a peer. We handled different projects for the same client. I had always felt his extroversion gave him greater confidence. So, I asked for his advice on a problem I was facing. The client kept scheduling work on weekends, and I was not assertive enough to avoid it. My colleague boasted that the client never called him on weekends and then, said in a bantering manner, 'maybe he just wants you to meet him on the weekends'. I knew it was not true, but I was still shocked at the insinuation. I remember being worried that if this is what he said to my face, what might he have been saying behind my back? I felt vulnerable that all the work I was doing could be dismissed and discounted so easily.

'Conscious and unconscious biases can be malicious in a competitive context. The perception of fairness and equity is an organizational issue to explore. We need to manage the perception with a degree of facts,' says R.R. Nair. 'We cannot become completely objective, but we want to be fair when building an institutional culture,' he says. It's easy to spot someone else's bias, particularly if you feel targeted by it. It's very difficult to notice and be aware of one's own biases.

Inclusion is culturally important to us. We all want to feel like we belong, and so exclusion is the most hurtful punishment we can endure. One way to avoid this is to suppress parts of one's personality at work situations. Rahul, a team leader at a technology firm in Delhi, says, 'The thin line between office and personal life should be maintained. I don't share my personal stuff with people in the office. If I do, I lie. I can't reveal my true personality at work. There is too much pressure at work and politics. We have to be diplomatic, know what to say and what not to say.'

Sonali and Ravi, a couple from Bombay say, 'We go out with our colleagues, but we don't share our personal life with them. They are our competition; we can't trust them.' Sonali adds, 'People are happy for you to go on vacation but if you leave work for them to do, they use it to create a misunderstanding between you and the boss. They are trying to push you aside to make place for themselves.'

Competitiveness is often seen positively from a business point of view. Some managers talk about how 'hungry' employees perform the best and motivate others to increase their performance levels to compete with them. Excessive competitiveness does not bode well for the teamwork and collaboration that is often required for business performance. How does a project turn out if people are manoeuvring from the start to appropriate all the credit and reassign any blame? Is it possible to function effectively in an environment of distrust and suspicion?

'Management which creates and encourages a collaborative approach will be able to be more productive and will bring down office politics and one-upmanship. This however does not mean that there is no favouritism at all,' says Ashok Capoor. We tend to like and dislike people for reasons that make sense to us but can be misinterpreted by others. The boss may feel his favourite is the one who performs best; others on his team may attribute other reasons for the preference.

On the surface, Indian offices seem to be friendly places where colleagues sit together for lunch, meet outside the office, attend each other's weddings and significant events. 'Casual socializing with colleagues and managers is considered a part of the work itself; but employees refrain from getting too close to them, especially with their boss/managers. This leads to a lonely work environment where they can only rely on themselves for survival,' says the research report by Quantum.

'My time is mine, for my friends and family. I can't spend twenty-four by seven with office people,' says Mohit. 'People used to dump their work on me and it used to bother me until I learned to smartly do the same thing to them. I avoid socializing with my boss because I know if he gets friendly with me then he will dump more of his work on me,' he adds.

I mentioned Ravi's conflict with his boss about working on Saturdays in the previous chapter. His is an unusually strong stance against a boss. I wonder if his boss might be more lenient if he understood the family situation. Ravi says, 'I can't confide in my boss. I don't want his sympathy now only so that he can take it out on me later during my performance appraisal.'

I understand this reluctance to share one's vulnerability. I hid my health condition for years because I feared being put to the side at work, not being considered a contender for any of the tough challenges that would eventually lead to promotion. It's only when the symptoms became too difficult to hide that I had to become open about it. It was a compulsion, not a choice, but I found more sympathy than I had expected. It made me wonder how much of my sense of vulnerability to workplace competitiveness was accurate and how much of it only my perception.

'When you feel that people don't connect with you at an emotional level, chances are high that you have kept your heart's doors closed to them,' says Rajesh Gangwani, executive coach and brand communications consultant. Almost every person I have spoken with has stories of people at work who did not understand or appreciate him or her. Office politics is always cast this way; the responsibility always belongs to the other. It is a rare few who have the awareness of their own accountability. The heart of all human conflict is the mirror response of dislike so entrenched that there is no telling who started it.

The survey I did on Google Forms from September–October 2021 shows that the pandemic situation has increased empathy levels for colleagues and there is some bonding happening through the shared crisis. Some respondents also mentioned that there is more reaching out for help and support through professional networks. Praneel, a senior manager in apparel retail in Bangalore, says, 'We did go through significant pressure during COVID-19, given the sector we are in. It brought us together as a team—peers as well as seniors and juniors. At the same time some colleagues could not take either the pressure or the financial impact of the pandemic and moved on.'

Praneel's team continued to work from office, as and when allowed, but people who have worked remotely through most of the last three years have missed personal interactions with peers and feel a sense of isolation. Chaitanya, who also works in Bangalore, says, 'Gone are the days where you could go to someone and solve an issue. Today we have to check calendars and wait for them to confirm. The answer would be the same with peers; it's a lot more transactional.' The layoffs and pay cuts during the pandemic have also increased job insecurity, which feeds into the threat perception and makes the sense of competition sharper.

Some companies are trying to address the problem of excessive competitiveness and office politics. Ritu, a senior manager at a global technology company, says, 'Our company is taking initiatives to try and build an inclusive culture. To encourage sharing ideas, experiences and suggestions on how we can collectively make the workplace more inclusive and less toxic, multiple conversations are being driven by the senior leadership team. Seeing our MD taking time out in an important all-India event to personally hold a session on unconscious bias helped me understand more about how I, myself, might be a perpetrator of misconceptions about other team members. I learnt a little bit about how I can work towards identifying unconscious biases that affect a person or group and deal with them better.'

The Quantum research report says, 'While entering the corporate world, employees are expected to put up a professional, guarded and impersonal image of themselves, which are mostly at odds with who they are.' While this is a dominant stressor at the start of a career, competitiveness remains intense at every stage of corporate life. For freshers, it's about proving one's worth by competing for the challenges and opportunities to do so. For the mid-level, it's about fighting for importance and promotions versus peers and relevance versus their juniors. For senior managers, it's territorial, maintaining and extending the boundaries of their influence.

Rahul, a team leader from Delhi, shares his thoughts on the motivation behind the constant competitiveness, 'I have friends who earn more money [and are] married but not happy. The mentality in India is that everyone wants to earn as much money as possible. People want to be famous on social media and get recognition as soon as possible; become CEO while still in their thirties.'

Social media is a good tool for a quick payoff and projecting the self-image we want to promote. It's the added satisfaction we get when someone admits his or her envy of us. The fancy food, fashion, cars and vacations don't bring us only the happiness of the experience; they transcend it to give us the brief hit of having exceeded expectations and getting ahead of the game for a while.

R.R. Nair is sceptical about the longevity of what he refers to as 'the external cosmetic appearances of happiness versus internal disgruntlement'. 'If our definition of success is limited to external rewards and excludes intangibles like connectedness, a sense of purpose and peace of mind, we desperately need a new dictionary,' says Kalyani Capoor. She adds, 'Life, instead of being a meaningful experience, is reduced to a constant and conscious performance waiting for applause. A perfect recipe for stress and loneliness.'

We spend so much of our time, and consequently, our lives at work. Does it have to be such a lonely and threatening environment? We are entitled to our own personal perspective on our lives and careers, but does it have to remain shut to all other angles of view?

I feel convinced from the research that no one sets out actively to be a villain to someone else. We are all trying to defend and promote ourselves. If someone is not playing by our rules or is oblivious to our concerns, do they have to become the enemy in our minds? Is it possible for us to shut down our competitiveness for brief intervals, to cooperate and collaborate for the greater good? Can business leaders find a way to tone down our cultural competitiveness for a safer, non-threatening and more productive work environment?

5

Jugaad @ Work

We corporate Indians are proud to own *jugaad*. It is widely accepted and respected in the global business world as a source of low-cost innovation. It is a magic mantra for profitability as it is expected to quickly produce high-value ideas. It sounds good, but this is not actually representative of what 'jugaad' is or where it comes from.

The word belongs to the rural north of India, referring to improvised vehicles made of random spare parts and materials cobbled together to work somehow. These are neither deliberate innovations nor the inventions of geniuses, but the desperate creations of people who have an urgent need but lack the resources to fulfil it. Our instinct for the ingenuity that has produced jugaad has developed amidst the background of colonial rule, poor governance, inadequate infrastructure and a paralysing bureaucracy that works better against us than for us. In practice, jugaad is a quick, immediate fix that buys time till a more permanent solution can be found.

The severity and duration of the COVID-19 pandemic has forced everyone across the world to hustle for immediate solutions—from doctors and vaccine makers to governments and businesses. Individuals and communities have had to be extremely resourceful to obtain medical access and supplies, especially amidst the shortages during India's brutal second wave of COVID-19. Against this backdrop, corporate employees have also struggled with additional responsibilities at work and at home, dealing with illness and loss, trying to cope with insecurity and grief. As my Google Forms survey from September–October 2021 shows, the work pressure has only increased rather than eased. Ajay, from Bangalore, says, 'Work pressure is on critical activities. More focus on immediacy and relevant projects.'

An increasing emphasis on the short-term has been the trend in Indian business for a while, even before the pandemic. Salary variables are linked to short-term results, people stay in one job for shorter durations and innovation cycle times are decreasing across industries. No wonder, jugaad is currently projected as the smart solution rather than only a temporary fix. We seem to be okay putting a Band-Aid on a bleeding wound rather than seeking medical help to cure it permanently.

In the previous chapters, I have mentioned the intense pressure and competition in the Indian corporate environment, the prevalence of conscious and unconscious biases as well as the critical importance of the hierarchy. These create an atmosphere of distance and distrust at work, which makes it quite difficult for us to own up to any weaknesses or ask for help. Jugaad or quick-fix thinking comes to our rescue in a very personal sense, when we feel we have no other recourse.

One of the toughest challenges in our hierarchy-driven culture is saying 'No' to a boss or senior colleague. Mohit, a twenty-something, who is in his first job with a travel start-up, has learnt this fairly early. He says, 'There was lot of workload on weekends, the other people on my team started saying, "we are out and so you do this work." They were loading the work on me. Eventually I started doing this too. I said, "I am not home, I am not carrying my laptop, there is a network issue, so you do your work." This is how I have to deal.'

Saloni, growth manager of an Indian start-up in Delhi, shares her experience of how she learnt to manage her work. Initially, the pressure to show she was working hard was difficult and overwhelming. When she looked for guidance, a busy senior told her to 'handle it however you want to handle it'. 'As I was getting to know my accounts,' she says, 'I slowly realized that you don't have to be after everybody all the time. Whoever is telling you about their issues should be helped, and if they are not saying anything, it means obviously either they are not working or they are working well. There are always other [types of] reminders, like automated mails, or if they are facing some problem, then their mails will be coming. So, checking their mails and only then calling or mailing them has reduced my work.'

R.R. Nair, says, 'Research has shown that there are four dominant learning styles. An individual can have a mix of two or more but it is not common for one person to be equally comfortable with all four. The first is the Activist style, where people learn by doing; the second, the Pragmatic style, which is about being instinctive and quick; the third is the Theoretic style, where people respond to data, concepts and frameworks and the last is the Reflective style, which is introspective and very time-intensive.' The Pragmatic style is most often required at work, where decisions and actions need some drive and urgency, and this is also where the jugaad-instinct fits.

Shyam, a general manager with a large consulting company in Bangalore, seems to have it all. I met him at his new apartment in a luxury housing project on the outskirts of the city. He is a corporate success, has a great lifestyle and a well-earned sense of balance. He is supported by his wife and mother. He shares many lessons as he reflects on his career journey, but one stands out for the passion with which he talks about it, 'We need to encourage smart working, not hard working. Hard working is for show, but it is not productive.'

Despite his obvious success, Shyam is cynical about the corporate world. His one experience of being laid off, much earlier in his career, is probably responsible for it. His conviction is that only performance matters, and it must be priority so you can either move up in the organization or move on. In his opinion, staying put is not an option and shows a marked lack of resourcefulness.

The Quantum research report identifies an emerging need for 'smart work' as more aligned with the corporate requirement of efficiency. It faces resistance in our culture because it is often viewed as an alternative to hard work, which is a deeply ingrained code. Smart working is more accepted and, in fact, expected at senior-management levels, where the decision-making and delegation powers lie, but at the lower levels there is more demand for diligence as bosses view it as a direct impact of their leadership. In this sense, smart work seems to be closely connected to jugaad, as a fix that works quickly but is not usually officially sanctioned.

Hard work is perceived as a requirement for the benefit of the organization, but smart work is perceived to be for the benefit of oneself, to progress in the corporate world and acts as protection against the stresses of overwork and office politics. We want to do it but it's difficult to own up to it. There seems to be an underlying fear of work being completed too quickly or easily. Perhaps, it makes us look redundant or we feel it will lead to work overload or we fear coming across as sly and/or lazy.

When I joined the corporate world as a management trainee, I was part of a formal induction programme on the standard operating procedures of the advertising business. It seemed simple enough, but when I started my actual work, I was confused. Every time I tried to follow procedure, I was laughed at. Neither the clients nor the production teams expected to adhere to the formal timelines, with each of their expectations at opposite ends of the spectrum. I felt like I was stuck in the hated childhood game of 'donkey in the middle', being bombarded from all sides. I studied the behaviour of my peers and seniors to learn that the actual ways of working were very different from the ones I had been taught. The production network was, quite often, just a piece of paper to keep the client feeling like they were in control. The actual timelines varied with how skilled the project lead was at pleading with or bullying the production studio. There would be several rounds of delays, with the blame being shifted around so it wouldn't stick to the project lead. When finally the project was delivered, all would be forgotten and the next round would begin.

Why would we have processes that don't work in practice? Sometimes the answer is glaring, like for some multinational companies that want to set global standards without considering local conditions. Sometimes the answer is less obvious, such as a few Indian companies where no one wants to question or debate the boss' understanding. Start-ups have a very high success rate in the first few years when they are led by young founders who learn by doing things themselves and who continue to stay close to the teams that do the work. These businesses often start to flounder when they are scaled up with speed, when additional funding comes with the pressure to professionalize and standardize their processes. Jugaad then becomes necessary when employees don't feel empowered or supported in doing their work and yet feel the constant pressure to perform.

'Jugaad or "hustle" has become a positive trait to be demonstrated in current times,' says Minaxi Indra, business leader and president, UpGrad for Business. 'In my experience it seems to be a glorified substitute for a lack of planning. As a business, while a hundred per cent certainty isn't possible, it can definitely be managed by process adherence and business planning. Escalations have unfortunately become a faster way to achieve the outcome rather than a last resort for help by the aggrieved team/party. In one of my previous sales roles, colleagues seen as hustlers were appreciated. They over-committed deliverables to customers and increased their deal sizes. This led to internal servicing teams being pushed against the wall to compensate for this over-commitment by either stretching, becoming "jugaado" themselves or raising exceptional approvals to deliver on the promised outcomes. Many a times jugaad is seen as a worthy synonym for being innovative while in reality it's anything but this.'

Escalations, in theory, are supposed to be exceptions. Clients or colleagues are meant to appeal to the higher-ups to turn up the pressure in case of gross incompetence or negligence. In practice, escalations are now so common and expected that they are part of the process. We appear to believe that things cannot happen without due pressure and escalation. Many stressed and stretched workers actually wait for the escalation to make the task a priority.

Ritu, senior manager at a global technology company, says, 'In one instance, the global finance team took a harsh stance against a demand of some of the partners to relax the company's credit terms. They did not want to give in and allow this to become the norm of their partner deals. This was, in part, also a test to check how many of the partners would accept this stance and how many would escalate their demands to the senior management. All the other countries accepted the stance, but partners in India continued to escalate it to the highest levels, so the terms were relaxed but only for India.'

I conducted a poll on LinkedIn in October 2020 to check the use of jugaad in Indian corporate culture based on people's personal experiences. It's interesting to note that the pattern of the results forms a bell curve, like a normal distribution. If we had a similar pattern with a much larger set of corresponding data, it would suggest that what we like to think of as a behavioural outlier or exception might actually be the norm.

I need to use some sort of jugaad while doing my work or to get my work done...
You can see how people vote. **Learn more**

Never	16%
Occasionally	44%
Frequently	24%
All the time	16%

25 votes • Poll closed

'When there is too much work pressure and politics, you have to be diplomatic. To know what to say or not to say—this is neither honest nor dishonest,' says Rahul, a team leader at a technology firm in Delhi. 'You have to be adaptable and change yourself to be able to work in the corporate world. I feel I got my first promotion because I changed my work ethic and mentality and I was also good with the office politics,' he adds.

Indians often have a flair for the dramatic. In our heads, we are the heroes of our very own Bollywood movies, which teach us that brute strength or honest intelligence can only take us so far. Victory requires a little more, something hatke (different). The Mahabharata is full of micro stories of rules being bent, avoided and even broken for the sake of a win. Reframing a moral or ethical breach as 'jugaad' makes it more palatable to the conscience.

Kabir, who works in sales for an up-and-coming travel start-up in Bangalore, says, 'I'm a Muslim, I don't drink. So, I don't go to bars, not even to meet up with potential clients. But, you know, my competitors would convince them to go to a bar, do whatever possible, give them whatever needed but see to it that their deal takes place. In fact, for competition, people have sent the wrong people to our property, and we've sent the worst people to their property.'

Kalyani Capoor says, 'A brain that's wired for threat perception, a work environment that's driven by pressure and a cultural conditioning that fosters competition often leave little, if any room for ethics. Neurologically speaking, this triad acts as a perfect trigger for the emergency response of fight, flee or freeze. The more evolved cortical centres of the brain are then hijacked and it's these cortical centres that regulate our moral judgement and ethical decisions.'

This is a reason why compliance is generally so difficult in India. We have a poor rating on the ease of doing business.[1] Layer that reality with processes and policies that are often designed for a theoretical fantasy. Add a few more layers for our competitive ambition, our eagerness to please the boss and a belief that we can only rely on our own ingenuity.

Ashok Capoor says, 'The bureaucracy and unpredictability of the Indian business environment make compliance with

---

[1] India is ranked 63 among 190 economies in the ease of doing business, according to the latest World Bank annual ratings. The rank of India improved to 63 in 2019 from 77 in 2018. Trading Economics:

https://tradingeconomics.com/india/ease-of-doing-business

global norms of doing business quite difficult. Business leaders need to set down clear guidelines that are sensitized to local business conditions and empower employees to adhere to them. If there is too much focus on short-term business deliverables alone, then compliance may likely suffer.'

The situation over the last two years has been reinforcing our need for, and our reliance on, jugaad. Yet, just as we now expect doctors, vaccine makers, governments and businesses to deliver us from this uncertain limbo to more sustainable and long-term solutions, we also need a macro perspective for our choices in life and at work.

Jugaad is not a skill. It is a compulsion. We have a historical preference to be subversive rather than petition unsympathetic authorities or to submit to systems we don't trust. We have developed jugaad rather than patience, driven by intense pressure, competitiveness and short-term thinking. Imagine the possibilities if the same ingenuity that drives jugaad was instead empowered to create real, long-lasting solutions that aligned purpose, people and profit for our businesses.

PART 2
LIFESTYLE COMPENSATIONS AND COMPULSIONS

6

The Carrot and the Stick

Deewar, a Bollywood film from 1975, has an iconic dialogue that is still quoted widely today. Amitabh Bachchan and Shashi Kapoor, playing estranged brothers, face off in this famous scene about their different life choices. '*Aaj mere paas building hai, property hai, bank balance hai, bangla hai, gaadi hai . . . kya hai tumhare pass*?' says Bachchan, playing the elder brother. By flaunting his wealth, property, cars and money as symbols of his success, he wants his brother to admit the rightness of his choices, though of course in pre-Emergency India such sudden wealth generation was not possible through any legal or ethical means. '*Mere paas maa hai*,' replies the righteous brother, citing their mother's approval to appeal to the Indian family values that put a mother's love above material wealth.

The cultural code of seeking parental approval is still deeply embedded in India. What earns their approval now is different since our liberalized economy does allow legal and ethical means to earn wealth. Education and career decisions are almost never taken individually since they impact the family's status and because, in most cases, family finances may also be taking care of expenses. Most parents, therefore, steer their children towards the path that leads to money, status and glamour rather than away from it.

Cheryl, manager of a large sales team based in Bombay, explains the attraction. 'With more money you will buy a house, you will look for a car, you will go for more luxury, so lifestyle [standards] increase. Earlier, I used to go to Sun City to watch a movie; now I go to Fun Republic. See, the standard is increasing. We have two televisions in the house. I have an oven that I use, maybe, once a week, but I wanted to have it because everybody has it. As you are earning more, you are investing in more things to upgrade your quality of life.'

Gopal, who works for an MNC based in the Delhi–NCR area, says, 'When I got my second promotion, I was really happy that I am going to get more money. We only see money; we don't see that we are getting more responsibilities. My shopping was increasing; that was the change in my personal life. Earlier I was wearing borrowed clothes, and now I was buying stuff for my family and friends, and for myself. I was happy that my income is increasing and so is my status.'

Corporate salaries and perks are perceived to be lavish in comparison to those of other jobs. Meeting the rising costs of living in Indian cities, providing for the medical care of elders, taking care of children's education and planning for one's retirement are the long-term benefits, while the opportunity to upgrade one's lifestyle is an immediate gratification, one that is enjoyed both at an intrinsic level and for its show-off value in society and on social media. Travel is a big part of this upgraded lifestyle. Foreign locations, distinctive experiences, luxury hotels and spas, exotic food and drink are seen as the rewards as well as the compensations of corporate careers.

HR expert R.R. Nair[1] says, 'Corporate salaries enable better lifestyles, and with most employees, there is a recognition that

[1] Leadership consultant and former Director-HR of Unilever group companies

their parents never had these luxuries. When they were young, their parents took them on frugal breaks, to a hill station or a hometown, carrying food prepared at home. When they compare their current lifestyles to what their parents went through, they feel guilty, and giving their parents expensive gifts and taking them on vacations is probably a way to deal with the guilt.'

When I was a young graduate, I was not sure about what I wanted. So, like many others in my situation, I looked to my parents for guidance. And like many other parents, mine steered me towards the path they knew best from their own experience. My father's corporate career had already given us a better lifestyle and many advantages, which I probably took for granted. I applied for a post-graduation course in management at my father's recommendation and when I completed it, it seemed my path was already set. My batch mates and peers were all applying for mainstream corporate jobs. So, when I set my sights on a career in advertising, it seemed like enough of a rebellion. The industry did not and still does not pay quite as well as other corporate sectors. This was the only argument that was used by my advisors and family to dissuade me. Job content, career growth, learning opportunities—none of these were part of their evaluation.

Many of the young women we met in the Quantum Consumer Solutions' research had, at some point of time, been drawn to the glamour of being an air hostess. Their parents discouraged them, worried for their safety and security. For them, a corporate job involved less physical labour, fairly regular timings—even for night shifts—and secure transportation services for women, either in the form of company perks or generous salaries. Naturally, this is where they directed their daughters. Cheryl, who did start her career with a prominent airline, says, 'After five years, I realized I am not growing anywhere, and I am doing the same job. Though my designation had changed, there was no change at work. And I realized that if I become some manager also, I will end up doing the same duty.' She's happy that she shifted sectors and feels justified when she sees some of her old colleagues check her in at the airport when she travels for her current job.

The attraction of a corporate job is not only confined to salary and perks but also extends to the promise of an even richer future, for it is seen as a sure step up on the success ladder. This is particularly attractive to youngsters, who want to keep their future options open. A starting job with a good company promises exposure, training, promotion opportunities, and adds value to the resume, enabling better career moves later with other companies. Multinational companies are perceived to have a distinct advantage over Indian companies and start-up businesses in terms of offering exposure to more diverse people and possible opportunities to move abroad, where salaries, work and lifestyles are presumed to be far better.

'In a multinational company, we have five to six rounds of interviews, then only we get the job,' says Devika, an accounts executive in Delhi. 'They take your personality, communication skills--everything--into consideration. It's not as if I am applying for accounts, so they will only see my accounting knowledge. They see other things too. But in domestic and start-up companies, they would just see whether I know accounts or not.' There is a distinct pride in her voice on having made the cut. Her friend Prerna, a financial analyst, says, 'We get to learn new things; our personality develops. There are so many departments, you speak to many people and you get an idea of every person. You get to know their mind-sets, thoughts are exchanged, and we learn a lot.'

'We can also flaunt in front of our relatives,' says Stuti, who lives in a large joint family. 'If we tell someone that we are working in this company, they get a good impression. Like, if someone says that my son has come from Canada, we can also flaunt with our company name.'

Psychotherapist Kalyani Capoor[2] says, 'While financial rewards and status surely are important elements of success, if they are the only defining criteria and if intangibles like healthy work environment, meaning and purpose, work-life balance are excluded from this definition, we are paving the way for burnouts and worse.'

Shyam, a general manager with a large consulting company, agrees that his vast experience has tempered his optimism. 'A corporate career comes with both plus and minus,' he says. 'The plus is you get a fancy life, with parties and swanky friends, but the negative is, there is no job guarantee. Today you come home from office and tomorrow morning, when you get up, you have no guarantee that you still have a job.' Shyam has had the experience of being laid off, and it was additionally traumatic because it happened when he had just taken a loan to purchase his home.

During the COVID-19 pandemic, several companies have announced layoffs and salary cuts and put bonuses and and increments on hold. The Google Forms survey from September–October 2021 indicates that job insecurity has increased. Maya says, 'Inflation went up to 10% in April/May this year. There's nobody who hasn't felt the need to tighten purse strings, even if one is financially well placed. There was a big fear of contracting the virus before the vaccines were out. Emotionally, the anticipation of loss and later coping with the loss of loved ones was exhausting. I know of many friends in their 30s, who have started consuming sleeping pills,

---

[2] Practicing psychotherapist for over 20 years, who also conducts mental health workshops for corporate set-ups

antidepressants, antianxiety medicines. Workwise, I feel it became more difficult to change jobs as though the job market has just come to a screeching standstill.'

'This pandemic has triggered a whole host of conversations about the purpose of life, work and one's own choices,' says R.R. Nair, 'but within the context of news and rumours about corporate layoffs.' Personal experience is not necessary to build on fear. No one wants to lose their corporate lifestyle perks — from flaunting their business cards and shopping recklessly to upgrading their homes, cars and vacations. There is also the pressure to keep up with one's peers. Losing a job means falling behind and the dread of never being able to catch up. This turns up the intense pressure and competition we feel.

Karan, a general manager with an Indian company in Bombay, says, 'The kind of expectations which are there from us, that is something which we cannot avoid. The problem is if you don't do it then there are a thousand other people behind you who can do it. So, we have to constantly live up to our management's expectations.'

'The corporate thinking is: I pay you so much so there is a time for you to come into the office but there is no set time for you to leave it. If you leave on time, they will make faces. If you stay on even though you have no work, then everything is good,' says Shyam.

Freshers tend to be more vocal about the stretched office timings and when work intrudes into their personal time, but they seem to feel the actual pinch less than their older colleagues. For younger people, partying and drinking are seen as good stress busters and the lack of time is a minor obstacle since most of their friends are in the same situation. Married people with children feel the lack of time more keenly because they are not often able to get relief on a stressful day.

'The interdependent culture of India also defines the way we work,' says the Quantum research report, referring to our precarious need to balance our individualist desires with our collectivist norms. We are constantly seeking to balance our own desires with those of our families and our own ambitions with those of our colleagues. When we compromise to make others happy, we might end up resenting them. On the other hand, if we put ourselves first, we might feel guilty.

It's a little easier to handle workplace stress when we can find support systems there, like Devika has built with a few senior colleagues who continue to mentor and guide her. She sees them as role models for her professional and personal life. However, across the research, perceptions of the office are not so friendly. In a gossip session in Bombay, mid-level managers share their complaints about office politics very openly—'They don't let each other grow. They will speak and do their setting with the boss and then, they will try to show you as incapable. They interfere in your work. When there are important emails, they don't mark you; they mark someone else. You feel left out that you are not participating in the work,' says Jai.

Despite the politics, competitiveness and pressures, corporate careers are still the preference. Corporate facilities like cafeterias, lounges and game areas are appreciated by youngsters but viewed more cynically by the more experienced. They are quick to notice any cost-cutting in these areas, but it is the slowing down of increments and promotions that hurt them far more. Benefits that extend to families, such as medical insurance and family picnics/travel are very attractive and help us compensate, to some extent, for the imbalance of time. Even the long hours, relentless travel and work stress can look glamorous from the outside because of the fancy offices, fashionable formal workwear, restaurant meals, business-class travel, five-star hotels that add to the feeling of importance and status perceptions. The glamour provides fodder for corporate war stories too.

Gopal says, 'Money is the only motivation for the corporate world.' Respondents to a poll[3] I conducted on LinkedIn in January 2021 agree that the main attraction is money:

I feel the biggest attraction of a corporate career in India is...
You can see how people vote. **Learn more**

Salary & Incentives	59%
Status & Designation	6%
Travel & Exposure	6%
Opportunities to Learn & Grow	29%

17 votes • Poll closed

Business consultant, Ashok Capoor[4] says, 'When I first joined work in the 1970s, the salaries were extremely low but the perks, like a house, car, telephone, club membership, etc., were good. By the time I was heading a big company, the new recruits were only interested in how much money they got in hand and were not really bothered about the perks. Of course, corporate salaries had gone up dramatically after liberalization of the economy and so had the opportunities for management graduates. Total money [salary] plays a very important role in getting good people to join and stay committed to a company.'

The pandemic has led to some adjustment of priorities with family and health becoming the top concerns. While many appreciate the improved quality of their immediate relationships,

---

3 https://www.linkedin.com/posts/profiledivyakhanna_insights-culturalintelligence-learning-activity-6747179676101439488-ubyV

4 Business consultant and former MD of Diageo-USL

there is also considerable fatigue from staying cooped up at home and a longing for the life before the disruption. The surge in travel as the lockdowns eased, which has been reported in the news as 'revenge tourism' is one symptom of this yearning for a more glamorous, misty-eyed version of the old normal. I suspect we are seeing such surges of revenge spending across many more sectors.

Our symbols of success—wealth, property, cars, impressive vacations and the luxurious lifestyle—require us to have money. Without it, we will lag behind in social status and future prospects. If the film *Deewar* were to be remade today, it might have to have a different storyline to be relatable. One where the brother who achieves wealth, whether through a corporate career or by setting up his own business, will also have his mother on his side and the one who disdains wealth, however noble his intentions may be, will be the failure who is able to offer his mother neither a comfortable life nor the respect of society.

7

Validation and Purpose

I compared corporate culture to an extensive buffet at the beginning of this book. While it is the size and variety of the buffet that are impressive and attractive, there is a very simple thing that can make or break the meal for us. The level of salt in the meal is critical to its taste. Chefs know that people's tastes could differ in what the optimum level of salt is, so salt shakers are easily available in restaurants. Money is the primary motivator for a corporate career, but money alone can only take us so far. There is something intangible, a personal sense of validation, that a corporate career provides, which acts as the salt, to keep us going and often helping us choose one job over another.

Sonali, a legal manager for a global company in Bombay, explains why she left a job at a large company that provided her several benefits. 'They gave me a proper maternity break. They gave me whatever time I needed to join back. My boss also insisted on not giving me a huge profile since my child was very small when I joined. He gave me a sorted profile where I need not slog for hours; I can take a day off; I can go out on leave. They were very adjusting at that point of time. They were thinking from the perspective of an employee. They were not trying to just get things out of me. They were not demanding a bigger output from me, but eventually that profile was not suiting me, because I am a legal manager.'

We tend to use our designations as our primary identities. They follow immediately after our names when we introduce ourselves to someone, and so we need them to represent us well.

It feels good to have a corporate job with an impressive designation and a great salary, but it feels even better to know that we fit in, that we have earned it and are deserving of the respect that comes with it. Getting paid a lot to do little is a nice fantasy we have, but it wouldn't be comfortable in reality. Imposter syndrome would kick in and leave us with a queasy feeling, as reported by many successful people as what happens when the timing or quantity of external appreciation feels out of sync with one's inner sense of accomplishment.

Kalyani Capoor says, 'The pursuit of success is as old as mankind. Setting a goal, working towards it, achieving it and celebrating the achievement, alter our brain chemistry by releasing happy chemicals of dopamine and serotonin. It's not the pursuit of success that's the problem; it's our definition of it. Defining it primarily by the pay cheque is an unhealthily skewed definition.'

Two of my friends and I started our careers together and have remained close, confiding in and relying on each other through our journeys. We have evolved to have very different approaches to our careers. One friend is on the career path—she doesn't particularly enjoy her job, but she has worked very hard to excel at it. She accepts that her chosen track is very demanding and she stretches herself to meet it every day of every year. My other friend is on the job path—through her experiences in different sectors in her early career, she came to believe that she would like her job to be just a job, where she does her work in a structured way and gets paid for it, without having to compromise too much of her personal life and time.

I have been on the passion path—I needed to have work that interests me and holds my attention, so I am able to put in the effort required.

Our approaches may be different, but we all have the need to succeed, to feel we have accomplished something of value beyond having a stable, well-paying job. These approaches are a reflection of our understanding of our motivations. We see choosing to prioritize what drives us as the only way that we can compete and succeed in a culture where we have to spend long hours and disproportionate effort at work. We all need to feel a sense of purpose, even though our definitions of it may vary.

Ashok Capoor says, 'In the 1970s, when I started my career, doing a job was in itself a purpose as opportunities were limited. The purpose was to look after yourself and later the needs of your family when you got married. You tried to bond with your colleagues and create a good work atmosphere because you were in it for the long haul.'

It is no secret that attrition has been increasing and job-hopping has become more frequent since liberalization opened up opportunities in our economy. While money and status motivations do drive this behaviour, there is enough anecdotal evidence to suggest that some people are also switching sectors in an effort to find more personally meaningful work.

The extended pandemic situation, while making it more difficult to switch jobs, is also helping many corporate employees derive a sense of purpose and meaning outside of their job content as per my survey on Google Forms from September–October 2021. Maya from Bombay says, 'I loved watching people reach out. I did it a lot myself. I made this a year for helping people, found jobs for families of COVID victims, secured medicines for patients, arranged provisions for lonely senior citizens and strays etc. I just felt like a more connected global citizen—in a very pure, selfless way. Even statements like "Commenting for Reach" on job-plea emails on LinkedIn had a positive emotional rub-off on me.'

'Today's personal circumstances are more favourable to pursue a sense of purpose as a validation of our choices,' says R.R. Nair. 'There is no lack of information. People are sharing their real-life experiences on social media, and there is no lack of choice. Earlier generations did not have so much information or much of a choice. This generation also has a far greater degree of financial cushioning; their parents have built up certain assets and have a smaller number of children. The earlier generations had to develop staying power and stamina,' he adds.

Staying power doesn't seem so important in building a resume today. Mohit who is in his first job in sales position at a travel start-up in Bombay is already thinking of where he might go next once he has completed two years. 'You have to make the right decision,' he says. 'The company might kick you out at any time. Then you will regret it and ask yourself why I didn't take that decision. So, it's better if you get a good opportunity [and] leave the company and go.' He doesn't hate his job but has observed his colleagues closely and feels this is the right way to build his career.

Mohit says, 'One thing I feel grateful for in my first job is that I learnt a lot of new things. In the corporate world, it is easy to get a good salary but I have learnt a lot of things and I am proud of it. When we are actually working and we get to learn, it is more fun than learning in college. Excel is basic, we know, but HQL and data sampling is something you come to know when you are working. And how to speak, when to speak, what to speak in front of which person is also a useful skill.'

The start-up work environment can be particularly attractive to people who are stimulated by challenges and bored by structure. 'The most interesting part is that I get to meet people who are like the who's who of the architecture industry. I meet architects, interior designers, builders and manufacturers. So it is interesting to meet these people and learn how they do things,' says Rashmi, who works in sales for a start-up in the architecture industry.

Saloni, growth manager with a travel start-up in Delhi, talks about how much she loves the variability of her current job. 'It was very boring for me to be in a desk job. I cannot sit on a chair and be on call for the entire day. I am not that kind of person. I also make reports; at times I make presentations. If these things are not there, the job will become very boring for me.'

Not everyone likes to work without structure. Large companies, whether Indian or multinational, offer a more structured environment with better-defined job boundaries and opportunities for fast-track growth.

Diya switched careers from hospitality to education, moving from a senior but hectic position to start again in a new sector. 'I questioned myself: what is important right now? My husband is earning well, and he can take care of me. His career is going great, and I [too] am earning. Moreover, I don't have to pay any bills or anything. Whatever I am earning, I am fine with it, even if I am earning ten to twenty thousand less. It doesn't matter because right now what I need is peace of mind.' Diya and her husband are thinking of having children, but that is not her only motivation for changing her career. She was burning out and was tired of the long shifts.

Our culturally defined gender roles make it easier and, sometimes, necessary for women to prioritize other aspects over money. Men face a lot more pressure to earn well. An advertising executive I worked with briefly gave me some insight. He wanted to get married and was going through the selection process through matrimonial agents and online platforms. He had connected with a woman, but it didn't work out only because she earned a higher salary than he did. He claims that this was a deal-breaker for her but not for him.

Preeti, a senior project manager with a multinational company in Delhi, says, 'When people come and say that they want to be part of my team because of the way I handle that team, it feels very good. Some of them have left the organization but keep calling me and saying that "I have never had a better mentor than you". That feels good.'

Appreciation is the highest form of validation. It tells us that we have been noticed and that our feeling of having secured the right job and our idea that we are doing it well and growing as professionals are not just in our imaginations but obvious to others. It is most meaningful when it comes from the boss and senior management, whose approval we tend to seek.

Organizations' responses to the COVID-19 crisis have also helped in making employees feel acknowledged and appreciated. 'The seniors are very concerned for the health of teammates, and this has ensured that we all care for each other too and work more closely as a team,' says Basant in the Google Forms survey. 'The care and concern of seniors help us perform better as we all feel cared for.'

The Quantum research team noticed a conflict between the Indian philosophy of karma yoga and Western-oriented corporate structures. 'The belief that one needs to put forth one's best efforts at work without expecting a reward in return manifests in the employee's life in many ways—hesitation to ask for rewards/raises/overtime payment, difficulty in negotiating on salaries and benefits and in saying "no" to extra work etc.,' says their report. 'However, the rising demands and pressure on the employee and the currently practised western idea of performance-based reward system leads to some conflict and tension. Employees find it difficult to draw a line between the two and usually struggle with this.'

The essence of karma yoga is encapsulated in a simple idea from the Bhagavad Gita —do your work without worrying about the fruits of your labour. However, the outcomes and rewards do matter in the corporate world, and we cannot ignore them. The material benefits that accrue from high performance are a clear signal of a job well done. On the contrary, not receiving the benefits is interpreted as a sign that we are not doing well enough to climb the next rung.

This is one of the issues I notice in the advertising industry. Salaries are low but there are people who still want to join the industry, with the belief that it will get better at a later stage. Attrition in the industry is extremely high at the mid-level as it is at this stage that people realise the salary gap vis-à-vis other industries is maintained. It is not just salary at an absolute level that is the issue but also the signals that it sends—that the work itself is not as valuable and there is a corresponding gap in social status and respect that results from low salary. Many, like the executive who wanted to improve his matrimonial prospects, end up leaving an industry they love because of financial obligations and social pressure

Money is the main attractor in corporate careers in India, but it serves multiple purposes, one of which is as a measure of our value or our progress or as validation of our choices. There are some who can do without this salt for a while, but in the end, there are so many choices in the buffet. We can sample some dishes and ask our friends to guide us on the others till we find our optimum level of salt.

8

Workaholism

When I was in college, my friends and I loved the American sitcom *Friends*. In one of the episodes, Rachael tries to smoke to fit in with her colleagues at a new job and not get left out of their discussions. I recalled this episode when I started working and found myself in a similar bind. Even though advertising had an almost equal number of men and women at the time I joined, many of us felt the pressure to smoke and drink to be seen as 'cool' and feel accepted. I had health issues that ruled out smoking and more than an occasional drink of alcohol, so I adopted an addiction that no one could shame me for—I became a workaholic.

Many of us have heard our parents and elders saying that work is worship. It's meant to be encouraging and is reflective of the respect due to work in Indian culture. Quantum's research report says, 'Work holds an elevated position and is considered a duty. According to Indian philosophy, work or duty is a sacred responsibility, which surpasses our immediate materialistic wants and helps in fulfilling the larger goal of life that is liberation.' It is translated as committing to work and prioritizing it over other aspects of life.

Krish, Omkar, Manu and Samar claim, in a gossip session in Delhi, that Indians have dedication towards work programmed into their DNA. They have been friends since their school days and are mid-level managers in different technology companies. Omkar says, 'It is in our DNA. When you go and check out the United States and other countries, you will see Indians who are working there will be [the ones] working on Saturdays and Sundays as well.' Krish says, 'If you want to give up on this and you talk to your family members, friends or anybody, they will say the same thing — "this is the time for you to work, at least until you are forty–forty-five years old, so keep on pushing yourself".'

'An Indian colleague of mine in London sent his junior an SMS on the weekend asking about the progress on his assignment,' says Ashok Capoor. 'The junior promptly went to the HR department with a complaint of harassment. My colleague had to give his junior a written apology to close the matter. This incident showed me the distinct difference between western and Indian work cultures.'

In a country with a history that glorifies sacrifice and martyrdom, work is a worthy cause, and there is a measure of pride in our attitude even as we complain of its burden.

Kabir, who works for a travel start-up in Bangalore, says, 'You will not believe it but some of my friends and I have deleted Facebook and till now we don't have it. Just because these small things make us perform better. You'll not see any other social media app in our phone other than LinkedIn, which is also for business purposes.'

'The thing is, people need to realize that if they've chosen to work, they have to be committed to the work like we are committed to our children. You must be really committed to your work, and you have to prove your worth there,' says Preeti, a senior project manager with a multinational company in Delhi.

The importance of hard work emerges in every research session and conversation I have had while working on this book. It is too obvious to be presented as an insight and yet, it is the foundation of every insight that is in here. It is our core belief that hard work is essential for success in any endeavour, that it needs to be visible for any recognition and that it is the duty we owe to anyone who employs us. Hard work itself may be rewarding for a few, but to most of us, this shared addiction is a compulsion and the only means to whatever ends we seek.

Sonali, a legal manager at a global company in Bombay, says, 'We are dedicated employees because being Indians we are very emotional about our job and our company. We give our best, but the company should also reciprocate in the same way—the way we think about the company, the company should also think about us. It should be employee friendly. But that culture is changing now. Companies are no longer employee-friendly; they are thinking of their benefits because of the size of our population. If we leave our company, the company will still run without us, but I don't know which other company will accept us.'

Deliberately plunging into workaholism is a strategy that works in the Indian corporate environment. Working too hard is not considered a fault, and there is more willingness to overlook failures or mistakes when they come from being overworked than if they are the result of inaction.

R.R. Nair says, 'There are three main factors that influence workaholic behaviour. One is the organizational dynamics—the life stage of the organization, the kind of sector it operates in, competitive pressures, etc. The next is the quality of interpersonal interactions—how much are you able to trust and rely on others, how controlling your boss is, the expectations from multiple stakeholders. The last and most critical are your personality traits and intra-personal dynamics, both often shaped subconsciously from your early childhood experiences. Some people have an acute sense of insecurity, a self-imposed need to prove they are indispensable. Some people are driven by perfectionism and stress themselves and their surroundings because of it. A few have a highly inflated notion of themselves and don't work well with teams, putting pressure on themselves to do it all.'

Companies in India appear to be enabling this addiction. Work hours are enforced only when entering the office; no one polices people who stay late. Everyone hates that Friday evening email that ruins a weekend but very few refrain from sending it. Oddly timed work emails and calls frequently start with an apology for the bad timing but continue to make their point. No one would report it as a case of harassment or expect it to be taken seriously. Working on weekends and holidays is the norm in many sectors.

Cheryl, who heads a big sales team for an international company in Bombay, says, 'In India, whether it is Saturday, Sunday, Diwali, whatever, we are working. [Even] when I'm on sick leave, my boss will say, "can you just do this work".' She also believes that people in other countries, particularly those in the developed Western world are better off. 'They are managing their personal and professional life very well; here, I feel, there is nothing like personal life or a very limited personal life. John [her husband, who is a doctor] . . . keeps getting calls and at night also he is busy with his phone. I too, from eight in the morning itself, start getting calls and they continue till the night. Even at ten in the night, I get calls,' she says.

To some extent, our obsession with hard work appears to be an acute fear of the opposite extreme. I recall having several conversations with my father before I quit my job to take a break. It's only when I had an outline of a plan, of some tasks to finish during the break, that we both felt comfortable with the idea. My own fear was also about giving into lethargy and becoming unemployable.

Kalyani Capoor believes we need to find the balance between working too much and too little. She says, 'Balance, in fact, is the key because the drifter who fails to honour his potential and utilize his talents and sleepwalks through a parasitic existence is as much out of balance as the neurotic workaholic who compulsively straps himself to a treadmill without a "stop" button.'

Ashok Capoor says, 'I always believe there is a difference between working smartly and efficiently versus working hard. I used to leave office by 5:30 p.m. and also encouraged my junior colleagues to leave on time and have a healthy work-life balance.' Our cultural discomfort with smart work as opposed to hard work is mentioned in Chapter 5. We seem to have a suspicion and lack of trust when things happen too easily or too quickly. And this is equally applicable to us as well as others.

Like me, many women use hard work to prove themselves as equals to their male colleagues. In my early career days, working from home was not an option. Working late nights and odd hours, which are the norms of the advertising industry, were not just exhausting but also stressful due to safety concerns. I once found myself personally delivering an urgent courier to the airport cargo department at four in the morning and suddenly realizing the situation's resemblance to the sets of certain misogynistic Bollywood movies of the 1980s. Nothing happened, but my fear in that moment of realization woke me up to the excessive risks I was taking.

Could I really change a collective mindset by putting myself in dangerous situations? One that already believes men are not just better workers but that they also deserve the lion's share of promotions and increments because they are the providers of their families? If anything had happened to me, wouldn't it just have reinforced their belief that they should have hired a man instead? Or was I trying to prove the point to myself by not availing the concession that the company would have made for my safety as a woman? Violence seems to have its own gender bias too and women are more vulnerable to it than men.

As mentioned in Chapter 3, our corporate culture is still guided by stereotypical gender roles—women are important to the home and family and men must work to bring in money. The gender pay gap reinforces this when couples plan their finances and lifestyle. According to a research paper by Rosa Abraham, Amit Basole and Surbhi Kesar of the Azim Premji University,[1] since the COVID-19 pandemic, women are seven times more likely to lose their jobs than men and eleven times more likely to not go back to work.

Work from home, which was a limited option available in only a few job sectors before the pandemic, was supposed to benefit women. Its enforced widespread adoption since the COVID-19 lockdown has revealed its difficulties, ones that both women and men face, as is clear from my Google Forms survey in September–October 2021. The boundaries between work and personal life have blurred further and neither work nor personal life can be switched off easily. There is no forced downtime from commuting and no real breaks for working parents. Neither women nor men can escape domestic chores and childcare by going to office. Nor can they ignore office calls and e-mails as the pressure to show that they are still working hard has intensified amidst fears of layoffs and redundancies. While technology makes us even more

---

[1] Priyanka Kakodkar, 'Women 11 times more likely to not work after Covid job loss', *Times of India*, 27 February 2021. Available at http://timesofindia.indiatimes.com/articleshow/81233013.cms?utm_source=contentofinterest&utm_medium=text&utm_campaign=cppst

accessible than before, it dilutes personal connections and makes professional relationships more transactional. There are conflicting data points about whether remote working makes people more productive or less and it seems to be determined by individual attitudes and work ethic. 'The ones who work are overworked and ones who chill are chilling more,' says Chander, a mid-level employee who works from home in Kerala.

Even in the pre-pandemic days, not everyone who had the option to work from home saw it as a benefit. Karan, a general manager at an Indian company in Bombay, says, 'We have work from home one day per week and that is not considered as a leave. Work from home one day a week is actually good. Having said that, at my work level, I don't do it because there are some expectations that I have to fulfil. It is ok for other employees.' His wife, Diya, can see the strain he suffers for work more clearly than he can admit. It's obvious to her. She says, 'He doesn't sleep at night. He is just thinking and, sometimes, he just wakes up and then he [is] continuously on the phone. And even after the phone call, at times, he never comes back . . . His mind is somewhere else.'

When I used to watch *Friends*, American culture was very far from Indian culture. Now, the distance seems to have reduced, at least in our cities and our corporate world. We have access to some of the same brands of fast food and fashion and some of the same benefits in corporate environments and policies. 'They are imitating,' says Omkar. 'Just bringing bean bags into office and having a cool environment does not give you the same structure.'

It's difficult to argue with this logic. Drinking coffee with our friends in Café Coffee Day and Barista was initially an imitation of our aspirations stemming from shows like *Friends*. It didn't change our characters and culture on a deeper level till we allowed some of our fundamental attitudes to shift. So, our workaholic culture is also unlikely to be changed by corporate policies until we work on our attitudes. Like any addiction, the first step is to admit we have it, and the next is to accept that it's hindering rather than helping us.

9

On the Seesaw with Work and Well-being

Sonali, whom I mentioned in some of the earlier chapters, has worked in various companies. She has a one-year-old child. Shortly after her child was born, she left a large multinational company to work for her current company, which is also global but has a much smaller range of operations. She says, 'Every company has its own culture, and it [also matters] where you work and how you work. Most Indian companies [want] maximum output from [their] employees and . . . value for the amount that [they] pay them. But when you go to any foreign-based company like my previous one, they have the culture embedded into them that you have to have work-life balance. Somewhere it is like a Key Result Area for you. You have to achieve work-life balance. They will give you lots of work, but at the same time, they will help you rejuvenate. But the thing is, you need to know how to do it. You need to have technology in place. You need to have manpower in place. You should have expertise . . . on how to do the same set of work in less time without stressing yourself.'

Sonali is right that many companies have good intentions and that it's up to employees to figure out their own sense of balance. Yet, it was while she was working for this enlightened company that she underwent a lot of stress. 'I wanted to conceive at that time,' she says. 'I was not able to conceive easily because of the work and time pressure. Now we are seeing a lot of our friends are also finding it difficult to conceive. They come to us and ask us [about] our experience and want us to recommend good doctors.'

Stress is the common by-product of our corporate lives. It manifests differently for each of us. Some people have headaches, others find their immunity weakening as they fall ill frequently, some people have severe acidity or elevated blood pressure, and some get stress-induced diabetes. Many people suffer from obesity due to overeating and/or drinking, ways in which they try to compensate for the stress, anxiety and depression they feel. In Sonali's case and for some of her friends, stress adversely affected their ability to conceive. Extreme cases of younger people having heart attacks are not unheard of.

'My colleague was forty years old. He could not handle the pressure at work, and he expired because of it. He died from heart issues. He was in sales and stressed about his markets. He had to travel a lot, was eating all kinds of food, had no time to exercise and all those issues,' says Jai, a mid-level banker in Bombay.

My own health condition was there even before I started working. It was so mild throughout my childhood that it was not bothersome enough to be investigated and treated seriously. It was when I completed my first year in business school that it all flared up. R.R. Nair, who also happens to be my father's friend, visited me on campus when I first arrived and gave me some crucial advice. I must learn, he told me, to manage both time and disappointment. The disappointment part was obvious, as it's difficult for high achievers to accept their limitations when they are being graded on a curve against some of the most intelligent people they will meet. The time part, I didn't understand at that point.

When we are young and healthy and away from our parents' house rules, avoiding exercise, skipping meals, eating junk food and staying awake all hours of the night don't seem like a big deal. In fact, they feel like freedom and independence. With a work overload, intense competitive pressure, and a library and computer centre that never closed, it felt like this is what we were expected to do. I was as reckless as everyone else, but I had to face the consequences much sooner.

The Quantum report shows that for most people, health concerns start becoming urgent towards mid-career and mid-life points and are often the reason for high attrition. Serious health conditions do not appear suddenly out of the blue. They creep up on us as we keep making the sacrifices that we feel are necessary for career success and ignoring our symptoms. Many doctors refer to these issues as lifestyle diseases. They cannot be cured but they can be managed and controlled through prescribed lifestyle changes, which entail exercise, proper diet and sleep routines that seem incompatible with our corporate work styles.

Jai is also a cricket lover and complains about how he rarely gets time to play cricket since he started his career ten years ago. His college friends in the session agree that exercise is the first casualty to the time demands of a corporate job. Nirav, who works in a multinational company, says, 'My weight is increasing as I am eating out more. That is what I have noticed in last two years. This creates health problems. We join the gym, and we pay for it, but we hardly go for a day or two and then stop. It is difficult to find time because the little free time we get, we want to spend with the family.'

Younger people seem less vulnerable to severe health problems, but they are very aware of the slippery slope they are headed towards. Most of them complain about not getting enough sleep. They are aware of not getting enough exercise, of their poor diet choices and yet, there seems to be a certain helplessness. They need to win the approval of seniors who have themselves been through this grind and continue to do so.

Rashmi, who works in sales for a start-up, says, 'My senior has been in this industry for long and she knows how it works. She can convince people. I am an introvert, so it takes me time to be able to fix meetings and get clients. Whereas she easily gets meetings and clients. I make more calls than her, but it just does not click, and she ends up getting clients every day. My bosses are very understanding, so they will not say anything as I am new. But I don't like it when I have not even one client in my weekly report. She will keep saying, "how come you don't get clients, don't do this, don't do that." It is bothering me and building stress. Sometimes, I have an emotional breakdown. I just cry when it crosses my threshold level.'

Her friend Chandini, who works for a global consulting company, agrees that work-related stress is impacting their physical and mental health. She says, 'We don't have time to give attention to our health or do anything for it, because we are thinking about these things. We will see ourselves very down, feeling low and lazy, our energy levels dropping consistently. There will not be any glow and shine on our faces, we are having more hair fall and headaches.'

R.R. Nair says, 'Money and competing to succeed in the rat race are the key motivators and this single-minded pursuit is causing people to experience a loss of control, a loss of purpose, and a huge level of stress and conflict. Companies are doing their level best to address and redress this issue. Senior management is under pressure to support their teams better as well as to leverage more from them.'

Making certain health-related goals part of the performance review can also cause undue stress, especially if they are a one-size-fits-all type and the work–related goals remain big and audacious. The pressure senior management is under is causing them more stress and this additional stress is also flowing downward, counteracting all the good they are trying to do.

'There was a time when I had good immunity. I used to be fit, and there was even a time when I was so fast. Office life gave me independence, but it could not give me health,' says Gopal. He has been working for the past eight years at a multinational company in Delhi, which he joined straight out of college. He used to be an athlete and played many sports before he started his career. 'In two-three years, I gained fifteen kilograms due to depression and anxiety,' he says. 'I was giving my one hundred per cent to office, but not to my personal life. I never did anything at home. I used to say that I am tired, I will not do any work at home, don't trouble me.' Over time, he had a realization that sent him back to the gym and towards his present fitness regimen. 'I changed my mentality, but the physical aspects had to be changed,' he says. 'It is important to be fit. I told myself, you are young. You have the energy, and in the future also, you must have energy.'

Nirav says, 'If you bring home your office work, that is mental stress.' He, Jai and their college friends admit that they rely on each other to deal with their work-related problems rather than share with their families, but they also try to discuss and do other things. Jai says, 'If we are discussing only office problems, that also leads to mental stress.'

'Our society and families place a high value on work. The constant pressure to outshine in the work environment causes stress and health issues and lack of healthy relationships with your immediate family,' says Ashok Capoor. 'It is of utmost importance that we maintain a good work-life balance as in reality, only that helps us to be more productive.'

With the persistence of the COVID-19 pandemic, immunity is on everyone's minds and work has crossed over all boundaries and has landed right at home, quite literally, in our laps. My survey on Google Forms in September–October 2021 shows that continuous working from home is also creating its own stress and impacting our health adversely.

Anshu from Hyderabad is relieved to now have a few working days in the office every week. He says, 'The ability to connect to people and drive buy-in [agreement] is lower when you don't meet in person; it's hard to read people's body language and their level of commitment. As a senior leader, connecting virtually was effective and efficient for the first year to eighteen months. After that, the diminishing marginal utility is fast setting in. Initially there was a fair amount of empathy. But the value of connecting virtually can never replace the face-to-face interaction; though I believe that in the future, it can be a mix of both. It seriously impacts mental health and well-being. We are social beings and need to engage with each other.'

'It has taken a considerable toll in terms of overall health, since most of my work has become sedentary and includes long hours in front of the screen,' says Sarika, who works from home in Bombay. 'There is a strong sense of screen exhaustion and overall fatigue that has set in.' Now there is no escaping work or the additional pressure of trying to manage work and personal responsibilities simultaneously. In a culture that believes in working all the time, breaks from it are even fewer and farther apart.

In his book *When: The Scientific Secrets of Perfect Timing*,[1] Daniel H. Pink mentions the difference that breaks can make towards improving performance. He writes, 'Vigilance

---

[1] Daniel H. Pink, *When: The Scientific Secrets of Perfect Timing*, (UK: Canongate Books Ltd., 2018).

breaks prevent deadly mistakes. Restorative breaks enhance performance. Lunches and naps help us elude the trough and get more and better work done in the afternoon. A growing body of science makes it clear: Breaks are not a sign of sloth but a sign of strength.' Most of us would feel guilty enough taking a break for lunch or an afternoon nap on the sly, let alone trying to justify it to a demanding employer.

The difficulty of switching off from work is something everyone relates to. Even when quantity of sleep is not a problem, the quality often is. I know my sleep is disturbed when I'm brooding over something work related. It's easy to say 'don't stress' and I've often been guilty of saying it myself. It's so much harder to try it and practically impossible to actually do it. My health condition, aggravated by stress, is also a cause of stress for me, as I'm sure Sonali's efforts to conceive were for her and Gopal's weight gain was for him. Stress seems to be much like a virus, reproducing and mutating before we can pin it down and try to win our freedom.

Kalyani Capoor says, 'Stress is experienced when the perceived challenge seems to far outweigh the perceived resources at our disposal. When this happens, the emergency response of fight, flight or freeze is triggered. Cortisol and adrenaline spike to combat and neutralize the threat. We meet the challenge and the emergency response having served its purpose shuts down. Let's look at this emergency response in its corporate context: External pressures in the form of intense competition, irrational demands from superiors, insane deadlines, thin or no boundaries between worktime and personal time and the lack of acknowledgement are by themselves probably enough to activate the emergency response. Add internal pressures of a perfectionist mindset and a fragile self-esteem to the mix, and the emergency response refuses to switch off. We remain in a constant state of alert arousal. This is when stress-related health issues, both mental and physical start to set in.'

We have our own internal pressures, some of which may be subconscious, like too low or too high self-esteem, perfectionist standards or a competitive streak. Added to that are the external pressures from family and friends, employers and colleagues, community and peers and the accepted social definitions of what success should look like. In chasing success, our belief in sacrifice and hard work is reinforced, leading to physical and mental compromises we make unthinkingly. We are constantly comparing ourselves to other people and they, too, are doing the same, each egging the other on in a never-ending competition. It is a no-win situation that becomes obvious only when our health deteriorates enough to interfere with our work. At that point, each of us must ask ourselves whether it was all worth the while and, accordingly, be satisfied, resigned or regretful.

10

Connecting Vs. Connections

When announcing my last promotion, my boss at the time joked that I must be a robot because no person could actually work in the obsessive manner in which I did. In a sense, he was right. I was behaving as if I was a robot. I did nothing but work, eat and sleep. My family barely saw me. I kept missing calls from my few friends. I only interacted with my colleagues about work. I didn't have the energy to invest in the relationships I was ignoring, but I know now that they were the only thing that could have reenergized me.

We Indians love to talk about how important family is to us. We have family homes, family cars, family friends and family functions. We like family outings, family vacations and watching movies that celebrate our family values. So, it's not surprising that all our respondents claim that family is their priority. What is surprising is that we allow this priority to be compromised so easily for the sake of our corporate careers.

'I don't make any commitments to my family,' says Mohit, who is in his first job with a travel start-up in Bombay, 'For example, if my family is planning an outing, I tell them not to make any programs that include me for the next three months and I say, 'If you are insisting on making these kind of plans, then you guys can go and I will not be joining you.' My parents often travel to Surat because my relatives stay there but though it is only a three to four hours journey, I still can't go.'

This seems harsh but it is a lesson Mohit has learned the hard way when he took his first vacation to attend his cousin's wedding in Surat. His boss kept calling him with urgent requests and he tried to work on them. Then he realized that he was neither able to focus on his work nor spend time with his family. He managed to negotiate with his boss to give the work to someone else before his parents' disappointment and his cousins' taunts became too painful, but he also learned that he must plan more carefully to minimize interruptions.

Interrupted vacations are a very common story, often even when planned in advance. Ravi, who works for a Japanese company, claims that with experience, one needs to develop a mature acceptance of this. He says, 'We get a leave travel allowance and we take it to go on vacation, but we also end up being busy with work on the phone. Sometimes, the children might complain. It's like you are physically here but mentally there. So, you are not able to enjoy the family or the vacation. But this is part and parcel of life. It is going to happen.' There is a sense of indebtedness here; the job that pays for the vacations must get precedence.

Karishma, a young media professional, also feels bad about the family events she has missed but what bothers her more is the daily strain. 'When I come back home, tired from work, I don't even feel like sitting and talking to my mom, to either tell her about my day or to ask how her day was,' she says, 'She will ask me what she can make for dinner. But, sometimes, I come home so tired that I will not even feel like eating dinner, I just crash. She feels bad that she has done everything for me and now I don't even want to eat. I also feel bad, but I am so dead that I just want my bed and want to sleep.'

Her friend, Rashmi, agrees that they tend to take out the stress of bad days at work on their parents and adversely affect that relationship. She wonders if it might be better if she were to take a transfer to another city. However, we find distance doesn't help the family relationship either when we meet Kajal, who is similar in age and profile to Karishma and Rashmi. She lives with a roommate in Bangalore, away from her family in Ahmedabad. 'I really miss my family at the end of the day because I feel lonely,' she says.

According to Quantum's research report, 'Being the provider to one's immediate family and relatives is one of the most important Dharmas in life, and Karma (work) is the means by which one is able to provide. This rationalization helps the employee stay determined to work hard.' Since work is seen as important for the family's sake, we allow it to supersede even those critical relationships. We depend on them to understand and forgive us since we do not feel we can expect the same from our employers.

Karishma had a steady boyfriend before she started working but the relationship did not survive once she started her career. She says, 'See, after work, you get really tired and don't feel like meeting anyone. I told him, "You might have had a light day, so you are in the mood to meet, but I don't want to meet you." And then he would say, "You need to understand how to adjust." Why should I adjust? So, I would just go home and crash, I would not even take his calls when I was tired. So, all this led to a lot of space issues and then finally I took the decision, and I broke up.'

Most of the young, single people we met had similar stories and these dating difficulties seem to lead to reluctance to get married soon. Manu, an Operations Manager in Delhi, whose breakup story is mentioned in Chapter 2, says, 'Both the parties should understand each other for the relationship to work. When they are both working, actually if they share the same work, they will know the things that happen.' His friend, Samar says, 'When you are in a relationship, it's very important to compromise right from the beginning and this should happen from both the ends. If it's coming from just one end, then it doesn't work at all.'

The married couples tend to demonstrate this sort of partnership, though their balance may not be quite equal but the alignment between them often is. They work actively to support each other and avail whatever help is available to them. Diya, who works in the education business and her husband Karan, who is a general manager at an Indian company, are a good example of this. Diya says, 'My mother-in-law is a blessing because she takes care of all the household work like the grocery bill, maid bill etc. She still handles it all and we are very happy. If she asks us to go and buy something, then we obviously do it.'

While Diya is happy that her mother-in-law runs the home, she realizes that she can't expect to have such a hands-off approach once they have children. 'Handling a baby is not a job, it requires a personal touch. I can pen to-dos to handle a job, but I can't pen down things to handle a baby,' she says.

Ravi and Sonali have a one-year-old child, and both work through the week, while Ravi's mother manages the child. He says, 'My mom also gets irritated at times. At least on the weekend, we must take care of our kid. Monday to Friday, she is there for us, but on Saturday and Sunday, we should step in, so that she can relax for two days.' 'And since after so much struggle, we got a kid,' says Sonali, 'we tend to indulge her in the little time we spend with her. I do not know whether we are ready to adjust completely to her needs.'

Rohan, a mid-level IT consultant in Delhi, wakes up at five in the morning to spend time with his four-year-old twin sons.

His wife is a schoolteacher and leaves the home early, so he takes charge of the boys till they leave for their school. 'If your personal life is not good, then it will affect your professional life as well,' he says, 'And if professional life is not good, then personal life also will not be good. So, they both go hand in hand; manage it well. It depends on your managing capacity. You need to manage it.'

Preeti and Varun live with his parents and their fifteen-year-old son. Their lives and careers have not been easy, but they seem to have found their balance. 'We have cultivated this attitude at our home that even my son knows that when some conference call is going on, he should not be disturbing daddy or mummy,' says Preeti, 'He just shuts the door or lowers the volume of the television because everybody is in agreement. They understand that this is important, and this is what work demands.' Varun says, 'When somebody has to work, it is not like you are avoiding time with the family. Even now if she has a call, then I will just sit with him or with my parents. If it is dinner time and she is not around, then I have my dinner with my parents and my son.'

While the family is expected to be understanding of the work commitment, they are not the confidantes when it comes to work pressures and issues. There is, on one hand, a reluctance to share the burden with family members and on the other hand, a conviction that they will not be able to understand and empathize. Only spouses are exempt from this but in general, there is a safe distance maintained for parents, siblings and children.

Mohit says, 'I don't feel like sharing my work life. Once I am at home, it is my time. At times, my mom will ask "how was your day at office?" But, I don't want to share anything with my parents, whatever I am going through. Whatever stress I am having, I don't want them to feel it too.'

'There are certain things we cannot share with our parents [but can more easily with friends],' says Karishma, 'We are stress busters for each other. Like we all are working, and we talk and gossip about our work with each other.'

Many respondents across the age cohorts mentioned their friends as their support systems for discussing work issues and pressures. In the gossip sessions, the group often pointed to one or more people as the default advisor for the others on career skills or moves or managing work conflicts. These safe and trusted friendships all predate their careers, having emerged from their school and/or college experiences. Despite the technology advantage of WhatsApp groups and social media, these friendships tend to suffer from geographical distance. Some in-person interactions seem to be required to sustain and develop the connection.

Karan and Diya are fortunate to have such friends living in the same neighbourhood, so they are able to meet them more often. 'We chill and talk, play games and go out for movies and picnics,' says Diya, 'Nowadays, we have started a new thing—we meet Saturday late night and watch a horror movie. And, then we make breakfast plans for Sunday morning.'

'With my childhood friend, I can talk about anything, whether work or personal issues,' says Karan, 'You can understand how it is after eighteen years. I have known him since before I met my wife, so you can imagine the amount of comfort I have with him. With my colleagues I only talk about work related things. We hardly talk about our personal lives. That is the difference.'

Diya says, 'People don't disclose some kind of things. They might have gone home and had fights because they had a bad day at work, but nobody wants to disclose that. It is like social media. Everyone wants to portray their happy sides.'

For most respondents, not getting time with their friends is a constant complaint. Geographical distance is compounded with the difficulty of coordinating busy schedules of work and family commitments. Mohit says, 'Yes, everyone is so busy in their life, either for their work or family. People are not able to dedicate their time to their friends. It is a harsh reality.'

While we may not be as fatalistic as we once were, we still operate with this sense that we must accept the situations we find ourselves in rather than try to change them. As we chase the big goals in our careers, we may not pay attention to the small compromises we make every day until they add up and begin to create their own strain.

I think I may have deliberately set out to be a robot when I decided early in my career that work would always come first. I was extremely introverted, anxious and uncomfortable around too many people. In my extroverted family, being preoccupied with work was also a handy excuse to avoid socializing. Once I started doing well at work, my sense of worth became too entangled with it. When I realized the impact it had had on my closest relationships, I initially felt powerless to change the direction I had set. It takes so little to damage a relationship and a lot to rebuild it. Many of us find it too intimidating to try.

We spend more time with our colleagues at work than we do with our closest family and friends. We know that having good connections and friendships can make our time at work more pleasant but there is a guard up in these relationships. 'Corporates are like the far-off relatives,' says Rashmi. 'You don't want to meet them, but you cannot ignore them. It is like you are not yourself when you are with them. You are fake with them, as a well-mannered person. You need to get along with everyone at your workplace.'

Karishma claims to have a couple of close friends at work, but she acknowledges that work is always looming over their interactions. She says, 'Sometimes we can party together and sometimes we don't come across or talk to each other for weeks. We just carry on with work and interact only when it is needed.'

When work is already a priority over one's family and prior friendships, it's natural for it to also overshadow any connections in the workplace. The underlying competitive pressures make for more superficial and transactional relationships at work. When there is a conflict in these relationships, we shy away from dealing with them head on. Some people may be overly aggressive and use their higher status to push their opinions, while others may be passive aggressive in saying one thing and doing another. Miscommunication means misunderstandings that never fully resolve, leading to the phenomenon we call 'office politics'.

Mohit says, 'One thing I learned is that some people have a bad memory, and some have a really good memory. So, share carefully about your family and personal life when you are at work.' 'If you don't keep distance, they take you for granted, they don't take you seriously,' says Rohan, 'Not initially, but over a period, the atmosphere will not be professional.'

Samar says, 'Colleagues are formalities. Some bonding may be there but then they all are competitors. They like to demotivate you and provoke you in any manner to gain the higher position. So, diplomacy, politics and jealousy are always there.'

'In corporate lives, relationships in the office develop as a need due to the long hours spent together,' says Ashok Capoor, 'However, these relationships are not real and reciprocal because self-interest comes first. If there is an opportunity for promotion or growth, some people may indulge in backstabbing and badmouthing to suit their goals.'

R.R. Nair says, 'In our time, we did not work with colleagues, we worked with friends. We used to carpool to work, we came from certain common backgrounds and shared together in company activities and overseas postings. This bonding gave us a community within the organization. Today, with people leaving organizations every few years, there is no stable community—this sense of anchorage is missing.'

The Google Forms survey from September–October 2021 shows how the COVID-19 pandemic is impacting our working relationships. Technology has enabled easier and more frequent group meetings, and there is a lot of empathy and support for people affected by the pandemic but as mentioned in the previous chapter, personal interactions seem to be critical and are missed. People who work in the essential service sectors and have continued working in offices through the crisis report closer team bonding. But those who have been working remotely report a greater sense of isolation and increasing distance in their team connections. New working relationships, in particular, seem very difficult to establish from a distance. Work from home is still the norm for some companies and social distancing is mandated for those who have returned to the office. Now that there is less possibility for spontaneous interactions, there is less scope for deeper connections.

Maya says, 'Socialising at work has gone amiss entirely. I miss dressing up and leaving for work. I miss my precious ritual of listening to my favourite songs while driving to work. I miss meeting friends, and the other fun and banter at work: the shared meals, celebration of milestones, looking forward to weekends, making presentations before a real audience etc. I sense an irritability and lack of patience in work calls and virtual meetings, which is no one's fault but hurts nevertheless.' 'We have lost collaborative working,' says Jhalak, a mid-level manager in Bangalore, 'I think working in silos will continue to exist and the pandemic has killed our people skills.'

To reach out and stay connected with extended family and friends, many of us have adopted the same platforms that have been developed to facilitate remote working. While we may get more quality time with our immediate family, our working from home and the stress we can no longer hide may also strain these connections. 'It impacts the non-working part of the family and is now an intrusion in their spaces and lives as compared to the past,' says Suveer, who is retired but continues to head his former company as chairman.

We know what we are missing out on and that makes the situation more tragic. Ravi says, 'In corporate life, the boss will always see you as an employee and will not be bothered about you. But when you come back home and your daughter smiles at you, you do not feel tired anymore.'

Kalyani Capoor says, 'Demands, delays and disappointments at work are inevitable, as inevitable as the microbes that dot our physical environment. And while we may never be able to sterilize the workplace to perfection, we can certainly build up our psychological immunity. One of the powerful ways we can boost our immunity is through connecting with others authentically and meaningfully. These connections, which offer us immunity against the stressors at work and would maximize our productivity, are the ones that are often the first casualties when we battle demands and deadlines at work. Even if work is our top priority and in fact, especially if it is, investing in building our immunity should be non-negotiable.'

Karan mentions that there is some understanding in companies that employees' priorities will change when they get married or have children. He says, 'Fortunately, we do have bosses who understand this kind of situation. Even if they don't, we have to put it in a subtle manner and make them understand that our priority has somewhat changed. Nobody in the corporate world nowadays would behave in such a way that they would completely lose focus on their work. So, everybody tries to understand that out of your hundred per cent effort probably the efforts will reduce to ninety or eighty per cent or maximum to seventy per cent. But I have not come across any of my colleagues who had stopped working or showed a complete lack of interest, and I am sure that I am not going to be that kind of a person either.'

Personal connections are valuable, we say, but we don't seem to be behaving as if they are. We are allowing our obsession with work to eat into the time we get with our family and friends. When we feel stressed, these relationships bear the burden of our moods and strain with the distance we create. We spend most of our time with our colleagues, but we don't trust them entirely. Our friendliness is on the surface and below that, we are wary just as they are of us. Our work environment does not feel like a safe space and cannot begin to make up for the personal connections we are sacrificing to our careers.

The urgency we feel to achieve is underlined by our understanding of the finite nature of our careers. We are hurtling to be the first to the finish line, but what do we expect when we get there? Do we expect our family and friends to forgive our neglect and celebrate our success or do we feel our work achievements alone will be compensation enough? Are we okay to take out this essence of our lives and live like we are robots?

PART 3

THE CORPORATE LIFECYCLE

11

Corporate Boot Camp

Siddharth's first job was an internship with a magazine, where his friend was working as a writer. He thought he would find his work in the photography department easy because of his creative personality, but as his internship progressed, he realized that a lot of hard work and discipline were required. He couldn't behave the way he did at college or at home. Every day and every interaction with his colleagues, whether good or bad, taught him valuable lessons. By the time his internship concluded and he was offered a permanent position, the change in him was visible to everyone who knew him. He had become much more responsible and confident.

Siddharth is not a respondent we met in the research but the lead character in the 2009 movie *Wake Up Sid*. Many of the respondents referred to this movie when talking about their initial experiences in the corporate world and how much they related to Sid and his journey, from being a selfish, indulgent child to a responsible adult.

'It hit me that I was so casual in asking my father for money earlier, but now when I am earning on my own, I realize its true value. I try to utilize it for the right things in life,' says Karishma, who works with a media company in Bombay. Saloni, a manager with a start-up in Delhi, says, 'In this movie,

I feel he was in a company where he was enjoying his work. It was a very helpful company. Likewise, my company also is a similar kind of organization. Yes, it is a larger organization but there is a personal touch also.'

In urban affluent India, the first job is often also our first milestone of adulthood. We enter a work environment as individuals who are expected to behave with a certain maturity and professionalism, even if, like Sid, we might at times feel confused, overwhelmed or apathetic. 'There is an apprehension about entering an unknown world, where we don't know the unspoken rules,' says R.R. Nair, HR expert. 'It slowly dissipates as we gain experience, and the unknown becomes known. Corporate orientations for each batch of new recruits are designed to help address this apprehension and enable them to form supportive bonds with others in the same situation.'

Fresh entrants are the ones most likely to notice and complain about the fault lines in our corporate culture—the long hours, intense pressure and workaholism, the lack of time and its impact on our health and relationships. The difference they report between their imagined expectations and their actual experiences remind me of something my grandfather, who retired from the army, used to say—the first experience of battle is a shock, no matter how rigorous one's training and discipline. Even the most reputed colleges and institutes cannot completely prepare their students for the culture shock they experience in their first corporate jobs.

Kajal, who works in Bangalore, says, 'People are a little artificial. There is competition and we really can't be ourselves. You have to be very sophisticated at work.' The respondents we met feel they were somewhat prepared for the hard work and long hours, having been put through the grind in their colleges and institutes, but their student life was so much more casual and simple.

Being late to college or even missing a morning class didn't feel like a big deal but waking up early and reaching the office on time is one of the major stress points for new recruits. Most companies monitor the arrival times physically or digitally and happen to come down hard, especially on freshers, for being late.

Even in the midst of academic competition in college, friends helped and supported each other. Progress, or lack thereof, was largely due to grades, attendance or some other rational explanation unlike the more subjective standards in play at offices, where personality and softer skills are also part of the evaluation. As long as college assignments were submitted on time, there was not much inquiry on whether they were worked on steadily through the semester or in a bout of panic the night before. At work, freshers feel they are under tremendous scrutiny most of the time and not just by their immediate bosses.

'Everyone around them is their boss, in a sense, as they hold a senior position, and there is intense competition between those at the same level,' says Quantum's research report. 'This further leads to a lonely work environment. While they [freshers] remould their personality to suit corporate expectations, their personal sense of self shrinks. A large number of employees express a huge loss of their identity (unique hobbies, interests, socialization levels, personality traits etc.,) soon after they enter the corporate world.' Most freshers feel the need to develop and wear a corporate persona; much like a soldier who must wear battle gear. Like armour, it is meant to be both protective of the individual's vulnerabilities and projective of the desired image that they believe will enable their success.

There seems to be a lot of external and internal pressure on the new recruits. They need to learn and master their job content. At the same time, they need to understand the corporate culture and dynamics to present themselves in the right sort of clothes and moderate their language and personalities. And they particularly need to learn to understand, develop and manage their relationships with their bosses and colleagues. Like the movie character, Sid, they can feel helpless and frustrated by having to figure these things out by themselves. The inhibition of personality is a gradual process and happens mostly by default rather than design as the recruits observe their senior colleagues and adjust to what they see being reinforced around them.

'After working hours, they are different; it is like we see two faces,' says Viraj, a trainee in a big consultancy in Bangalore. Kajal agrees and says, 'They might really put you down in the office but outside, they offer you a coffee. Sometimes we are confused [whether] to say yes or no, but at the end, we say why not. It is like now we are trained; office is office and outside is different, so we see two faces of the people everywhere.'

Psychotherapist, Kalyani Capoor says, 'Taking up the first job is an important life stage transition. It would throw up understandable transitional stress for the freshers since life is no more as they knew it to be. This stress is easier to handle when they enter this alien world expecting life to change. Having a helpful mentor goes a very long way in making this transition smooth. Being equipped with a healthy sense of self-esteem acts like emotional immunity, allowing the fresher to interpret and act upon the stressors in the most functional of ways. Our self-view and world-view act as invisible but powerful filters through which we interpret data and act upon it.'

'There will be politics, but they never say what kind of politics . . . in my team, everybody is a senior and there is pressure on everybody,' says Viraj. 'Almost everybody has done four, five, seven and eight years of work and whatever ideas I give, they say it will not work. But then they will give my idea as theirs to different teams.'

Viraj appears unclear and unsure about the boundaries of right and wrong in his workplace. Many of us, including some of his seniors, may see his ideas being appropriated as outright cheating but he calls it 'politics'. Given their low status in the corporate hierarchy, most freshers feel reluctant to speak out or take a clear stance against a senior colleague. In the research project, we heard many stories from the respondents about being assigned unimportant and mechanical jobs, not being appreciated for good work and others stealing credit for their ideas, exactly what happened with Viraj. They also have stories of being guided and supported. Chandini, who works in a consulting company in Bombay, says, 'There are some good people too, like my boss. When you do something wrong, she will not shout at you in front of others; she will come and talk to you and understand why you did it wrong and tell you how you should now correct it. I love that thing about corporate life, there are a few people who are an inspiration for me.'

My friend and fellow planner, Jasravee Kaur Chandra is director of brand building, research and innovation at Master Sun. She says, 'When you take up a new job, the advice is to observe the culture first. Learn as you step in, like a bride getting into a new family. You figure out the power equations, you figure out who does what—you know, without disturbing anything, you just adjust and accommodate and then at some point, when you will be handed over the keys, you can see what you want to do.'

'Adjust and accommodate' is the preferred Indian attitude to anything new. We pride ourselves on being flexible enough to fit into whatever the situation is. And this is the advice families tend to give their children, while they also encourage them to explore new sectors, companies and jobs that didn't exist a few years earlier. So, not having a clear frame of reference, many freshers try to observe and understand the unspoken rules of right and wrong in their workplace before they feel confident enough to speak up for themselves.

Mohit has a sales job with a start-up in the travel industry in Bombay. He says, 'My friend told me, "Why do you always say yes to everyone? Why don't you ever say no?" I was scared that they would take some action if I did. At the back of my mind, I knew that if I give some genuine reason for saying no, then I don't think anyone would do anything. One thing I learned is that when you learn to say no, it helps you. Like, if anyone in your organization asks you for something and if you always say yes, then you become like a donkey carrying a lot of load on your back. So, you should learn the art of saying no. I learnt it and now it is okay, my work is manageable.'

Raghav, a data operator in Bangalore, works in a company where some of his cousins are senior managers. He appreciates their guidance in navigating the workplace and also understands that their relationship within it has to be different. He says, 'They talk whatever they feel but I have to understand that they are my managers. We will also behave like this with our juniors.'

It's difficult to know whom to trust and whom to be wary of. This is a sense that develops only through experience. The challenge is multiplied if this experience is to be gained largely through remote working, as it has been the case through most of the pandemic. As mentioned in the previous chapter, new working relationships are particularly difficult to establish through technology alone and freshers would find it even more challenging since they need to observe and mimic their senior colleagues very closely to feel like they fit in.

Freshers naturally gravitate towards those bosses and colleagues who they feel a connection with and try to emulate them. They get a glimpse of what they might expect by observing how their role models fare in the corporate hierarchy and how they are treated by the company.

Leaders looking to shape and influence the next generation would know that their decisions send signals to their employees on the kinds of behaviour that will see them rewarded and promoted and those that won't. In Chapter 4, Mohit shared his disillusionment with his company when he saw a colleague whom he liked and respected being treated badly and passed over for promotion. That colleague left the company and Mohit has decided that he will also move once he completes two years, partly due to this. His closeness and identification with his colleague make him worry that he might face similar treatment if he stays.

As R.R. Nair pointed out in the earlier chapter, there is a missing sense of anchorage in many organizations because of the lack of a stable working community. Employees tend to change jobs and companies every few years and companies themselves seem more focused on bringing in new talent rather than investing in training and retaining existing employees. Most new recruits know that they are entering a shifting landscape, aware that not only will it keep changing but that they, too, will probably move to broader horizons. Across the research, respondents shared their belief that loyalty is not a value that is reinforced by current corporate policies. Many senior managers might say this is merely a response to the lack of loyalty in employees today. Like the chicken and egg syndrome, we might never resolve how it started, but whose onus is it to try to break the cycle?

The advertising industry in India is a small sector and deliberately projects an anti-corporate image. There is a flatter hierarchy, relaxed codes on dress and language and a lot of informality in the work environment. This, along with some perceptions of glamour, initially attracts new recruits. We see a diverse mix of creative, curious and passionate people enter the workforce each year but an almost equal number of them quit the industry within two years. Despite the informality, the work is very demanding and subject to intense pressure on deliveries and timelines. Because of the informality, there is a sense of chaos and blurring of job and people boundaries. There is less time and money to invest in training, and salaries are at the lowest end of the corporate spectrum. Eventually, the informality does not seem an adequate compensation for the lack of money and status.

Is it a coincidence that the highest starting salaries are in investment banking and consulting, which are at the extremes of formality in the spectrum of corporate India? New recruits in these sectors are given strict guidelines to follow and dress allowances as part of their induction. Since status in our corporate culture follows money, the hierarchy of sectors is clearly understood even by new recruits. They feel forced to make a choice but deliberately giving up money and status goes against all our cultural codes. It's not a surprise, then, that so many young people are gravitating to start-up jobs, which often combine an informal college atmosphere with the promise of a payday when the organization reaches the stage of an initial public offering (IPO). Well-funded start-ups like the ones Mohit and Saloni work for also give them good designations and competitive salaries.

With technology becoming more integrated into our work lives, many freshers have an unexpected advantage. Karishma says of her seniors in a media company in Bombay, 'They don't know how to use technology the right way. When there is a gap in technology skills, they come to us millennials and ask for help.' Many companies are encouraging reverse mentoring, setting aside the hierarchy for informal sessions where the freshers get to teach their seniors.

Personal insecurity and a lack of experience make freshers feel like they must compromise their interests and personalities for the right first job. 'I don't like it, but once I get to some level in my career, then I will also understand how things work. Right now I am only settling into things; then it will get better,' says Rashmi, inadvertently echoing Jasravee Kaur Chandra. Once her first job with a start-up in Bombay lays the foundation for her resume and gives her enough battle experience, she will feel more confident of progressing in the direction of her true aspirations.

Business consultant, Ashok Capoor says, 'Earlier HR departments used to concentrate on creating loyalty and stickiness amongst the employees and spent a great deal of time and effort on nurturing and training talent. However, now, loyalty seems to have become a lower priority and cost controls are important. Because of this, the relationship between companies and employees has become more transactional. The companies hire people with less experience and less salary to replace the people who leave. Thus, the overall quality of the manpower is getting diluted at lower costs. The fresh employees also tend to see large companies as a stepping-stone for getting better salaries. The short term has become more important than the long term, which in my opinion has an adverse impact on the quality of manpower and loyalty. The continuity in the business suffers due to this.'

Families seem equally supportive and actively encouraging of ambition for both women and men at this stage of their careers. For most men, the pressure to succeed is non-negotiable. They are encouraged to work hard and progress quickly; leaving one job is only acceptable when it's for another with even better prospects. For most women, the pressure to succeed is tempered with some expectations of flexibility and planning for the eventuality of marriage. While fathers tend to support their ambitions more wholeheartedly, the mothers often provide their daughters a reality check, using their own life experience to anticipate the issues that might crop up with future family and childcare responsibilities.

Many women get their first taste of 'real' independence on getting their first corporate job. Family rules imposed on them are relaxed in favour of the demands of their jobs and employers. From working late to travelling, from not having to justify their purchases to making personal investments, their self-confidence and self-worth become stronger. 'What will people say' has been a common refrain their parents have used against them to deny freedom, but once there is a corporate job with a status to flaunt, parents' attitudes also change. It appears to give them more confidence in their daughters' abilities to handle different situations and they also seem to become less sensitive to gossip. Perhaps, they feel their daughters are now responsible adults and need not be overprotected anymore.

Chandini says, 'I want to be an independent woman and do things on my own. Having a fall-back option will be a good thing to have, a kind of financial cushion if things don't work for me after marriage or if I need to take a longer maternity leave or whatever. To have someone who can support you is good, but . . . it is also good being able to do things on your own, having a choice of spending how you want to spend. If I don't work after marriage [and] want to give my parents something or even if I have to give something to my in-laws, I don't want to be dependent on my husband for [that] money.'

Saloni credits her family for supporting her career and not putting traditional demands as obstacles in her way. She is also in a steady relationship and says her boyfriend is most encouraging of her career and her plans to be an entrepreneur in the future, giving her advice when she needs it. While she is not too keen on marriage, he is, and she knows that they will inevitably get married. She says, 'Marriage is required because there will be pressure on him, his family and my family as well.'

When we ask Saloni if she thinks her career plans might change after marriage, she tells us about her boyfriend's sister. 'She is a little scared and does not want to do a flexible job. So, they want her to be more open and broad-minded. He told me that they want her to be independent like me. So, I feel his family is supportive. I do not think that they will financially support any business I start but they will support me emotionally.'

As mentioned in the previous chapter, most young people struggle with dating at this stage. With so much time spent at work, there is a strain on existing relationships, and meeting new people outside of work is rare. There seems to be a difference of opinion between the genders on flirting with and/or dating colleagues. The men seem quite open and willing, but women tend to be more cautious, protective of their reputations in the office and careful with the trust of their families. There is an underlying fear of being misunderstood and harassed, given the culture of victim blaming that prevails in society. They have also been put on guard on account of the stories and gossip they have heard.

'We should not make any boyfriends in the office,' says Stuti, an executive with an IT company in Delhi. 'If we smile and talk to someone, there will be a misunderstanding and people will start gossiping about us.' Chandini says, 'I come from a community where there are very few girls working, so I want to represent to my community that girls can work. I have to grow in my field, and I have to show that even as a girl I can work and grow, and it should continue after my marriage also.'

Saloni, Karishma, Mohit and the other freshers we met feel motivated and encouraged to work especially hard by their families and communities due to the cultural pressures discussed earlier. They also seem to be driven by their insecurities to learn, grow and contribute quickly. Their perceptions of what going higher up the ladder will do to make their work and personal lives easier also play a role. They have a rose-tinted view of promotion and everything, they believe, that comes with it—delegation, work-life balance, higher salaries and luxurious lifestyles. They believe that just a step or two up the ladder will make a big difference.

'I think after a time they have juniors working for them, so they don't have to do all the slogging; they divide the work within their juniors, so it becomes easier for them. They are not the only ones doing everything, they have everyone working and they just go through everything and rectify if there are any mistakes, so it is much easier on them,' says Rashmi of her senior colleagues. Chandini says, 'They go for expensive holidays. They go to Europe . . . They always travel abroad.' Karishma says, 'All this is because they earn so much, so they can afford to splurge on all this not just for themselves, but for the whole family. It is also about where they shop and what they buy, they can afford the most luxurious lifestyle'.

Quantum's research report says, 'Their quest for progress and upward mobility takes precedence over everything else at this stage. Additionally, at the beginning of one's career, an employee is expected to show immense gratitude for the opportunity to work, which further leads to a culture of unquestioned subservience.'

If we look at the current corporate employees with five or less years of experience as a collective, they have a lot going for them. For one, they are well connected as a cohort on social media and group platforms and can easily access information on different jobs and companies. Then, they are far savvier with technology than their bosses and senior colleagues, who often refer to them for help. They have been brought up in increasingly democratic homes, so they feel able to assert themselves and question rules that don't suit them once they are a little comfortable with the work environment. Yet, despite being quick learners, they feel uncertain about how to gauge their bosses and colleagues, to know who to trust and who to be wary of. They are made to feel conscious of being at the bottom of the hierarchy and insecure about the competition they face. When this cohort works on suppressing their personalities, they are also repressing some valuable parts of themselves that might have helped our corporate culture become more authentic, real and human. At present, they feel they have little choice but with a bit more experience, they would like to be more autonomous and have more flexibility over their work and lives. Wouldn't we all?

12

Middle of the Marathon

Scott Douglas is a journalist and author whose areas of expertise are running, fitness and health. In 2020, he wrote an article that featured on the Runner's World website, offering tips to marathon runners[1]. 'No matter how much you're raring to go, keep things under control until well past the halfway mark. Then you can start racing,' he says. This is critical advice to be able to stay on course and complete the race. For a shorter sprint, a runner might apply a different strategy but pacing oneself is essential for a marathon.

The freshers we meet are already on a sprint, motivated by the belief that their immediate bosses and seniors in the middle of the corporate journey have it much easier. They push themselves hard to get a few steps up the ladder, thinking they can then pause to catch their breath. Do a few more years of experience and exposure to the corporate world really make such a big difference?

---

1 Scott Douglas, 'Marathon Runners Need These 26 Tips to Crush 26.2 Miles', *Runner's World*, 15 August 2020. Available at https://www.runnersworld.com/training/a20808326/26-tips-for-running-your-best-26-2/

The mid-level respondents we met appear to be more confident and comfortable with the corporate world. They have the air of battle-ready soldiers, who know what they are up against. Their corporate persona is more developed and worn less self-consciously. They know some of the rules of the corporate game by now and have a fair idea of how well they might be at playing it.

Cheryl, who heads a big sales team in Bombay, says, 'My responsibilities increased with this promotion. I used to send a report to my manager, but now I have to collate all the reports. I am creating more reports for my support departments. Earlier I was responsible for only my performance, like I had to justify why I have failed or how I did better. Now, I have to justify for my entire team. So, if fifteen people are doing well and one is not, I have to give that person a push, to understand why they are failing. I am responsible for all of them.'

Gopal has been working in the same multinational company in Delhi that he joined after graduating almost a decade ago. He feels that his promotions have not made his work-life as easy as he thought they would when he was a fresher. 'After you reach a certain level, you have to work on whatever [technical] system you get, and you cannot give any excuse,' he says. 'If they are giving you a promotion, they also expect a lot more from you.

Cheryl has her eyes firmly set on her next career milestone and is optimistic about achieving it owing to her past success. She realizes that she may face some difficulties, especially if and when she and her husband decide to have children but is confident of negotiating a way forward even if it means changing her job function or working for another company. Gopal is also working towards the next milestone but simultaneously adjusting his expectations by questioning what it really means to him. He doesn't seem as confident of getting there. Cheryl seems happy with her career, but Gopal seems resigned.

'I know people who have a good work-life balance. The thing is that they are married, and their wives are also working, and they are staying away from their parents,' Gopal says. 'Throughout the day, both are working, and when they reach home, they help each other. When there are more members in the family, maybe kids or parents, then it is difficult. I have friends who are not able to strike this balance. They are struggling.' Gopal is not married yet, but he seems to be anticipating issues.

For many of our respondents, this stage in their career is challenging on multiple levels. They are in transition from performing their jobs to managing a team's performance, from trying to learn from their own mistakes to seeking to correct the mistakes of others. Their elevation in status leads them to more exposure to senior management and clients and moves them from working behind the scenes to frontstage. And while they are trying to cope with these transitions at work, some of them are also going through big changes in their personal lives—shouldering increased family responsibilities, with marriage and children, and caring for ageing parents nearing retirement.

'Previously you just had to manage your work and your parents were doing everything. Now you have to manage yourself and your family. You have to take permission from your spouse for most things,' says Jai, who works in a bank in Bombay. His wife is a homemaker, and the couple live with Jai's parents.

Jai's friends from college, Hetal and Anvi, are also married and work at mid-level corporate positions. They feel supported in their careers by their husbands and in-laws. 'The new mothers-in-law are all open minded,' says Anvi, 'There are huge differences from before.' Hetal says, 'They are very understanding. Today, mothers-in-law are also busy with their own lives.' Hetal and Anvi feel free from the traditional restraints that might have been applied to limit their careers, yet they have a sense of some boundaries. Anvi says, 'We have to keep in mind where and how the husband is working and we cannot move abroad.'

Sonia and Kabir live independently from either of their parents in Bangalore. They found marriage a tough transition even though they knew and dated each other from when they were in school. 'It was difficult for me because I had to handle the house and my work also,' says Sonia. 'I had never done any housework before. My mom used to even serve food on my plate. So you know, after coming home from work I had to cook, when before, I used to just order my mom to keep my food ready. It was stressful.' Kabir helped her with the cooking initially. He says, 'Our understanding has grown a lot from that phase. Though we dated, after marriage it was like we didn't know each other at all. But now it is like we know each other.' Sonia says, 'Staying in a nuclear family, you know, that's the whole thing that makes your marriage. It gives you time to think what he wants, what I want, there are no distractions.'

Sonia has recently given up her hectic design career to move into the human resources field as they are planning to start a family. She and Kabir claim to consult with each other on their career decisions. Kabir says, 'Even though I am more experienced than her in the corporate field, sometimes in discussion with her, I end up getting some good solutions.' Yet, he did forget to tell her when he took up his current assignment. 'It was not that maybe she had a doubt. The larger picture was this: I was really busy those days, I didn't have the time to consult, inform and all that,' he says.

In Chapter 10, I mentioned Ravi and Sonali's childcare arrangement with his mother. She looks after the young child through the week so they can focus on their jobs, and they take over parenting responsibilities on the weekends. Ravi says,

'Now there is no difference between male and female, because she has done her education. Her career is also important for her. She has some dreams. I cannot stop her from doing that. If she wants to fly, she can. Even with regard to the baby, we planned together. So, it is our equal responsibility.'

Sonali is excited in anticipation of a work-related conference that she's going to travel for when we meet her. This will be her first since her pregnancy, and she knows that with a small child, her travel options will continue to be limited in the near future.

Manu, Onkar, Krish and Samar have been friends since they went to school together. Onkar is the odd man out in the group—he works in human resources while the others have technical jobs, and he is the only one who is married. Some single men believe that women are given too many privileges and concessions at work, and this makes them resent and doubt their abilities. The #MeToo movement has also left them unsure and made them cautious. Krish says, 'I know so many girls who know nothing but they get hired because of their personality and their appearance. And their work will have to be done by so many guys. Someone else will have to work and they are profiting because of that.' Samar says, 'We too have families. Maternity leaves are generous. Everything is work-from-home for them. We are suffering because we are men.' Onkar is the lone dissenter in the group who does not see women at work as a threat. It is ironic because he has more women colleagues and the others, by their own admission, have very few.

The mid-level corporate men we met tend to be more extreme in their views of gender stereotypes—either idealistic about empowerment like Ravi or chauvinistic like Samar and Krish. The women we met tend to have a more practical and realistic view. They acknowledge that their husbands' career prospects are more significant to their families' future. They willingly accept the larger share of the family and childcare responsibilities. They invest in their careers but seem to prioritize the returns they get from their families as this comes more naturally to them, due to the deep-rooted gender biases, which disproportionately reward women at home and men at work.

Kalyani Capoor says, 'More often than not women allow themselves to take it a bit easier at this stage than their male counterparts. The same cultural conditioning that demands that men make their career their topmost priority, permits, encourages, even pushes women to slow down a bit at work and focus on starting and nurturing a family.' Women are also bearing the larger share of the increased childcare and household responsibilities in the COVID-19 pandemic.

Among the men whom we met, there is a feeling of 'missing out'. Yes, they can more easily get out of family responsibilities, but this also seems to hurt them at some level, almost as if their presence at home is not really required and can be compensated for by their career status and salaries.

Ravi says, 'Yes, money is important. But . . . once you will be in the corporate world . . . plus–minus two lakhs is okay. No problem. But I want peace of mind and quality time with my daughter.'

'I don't get time to meet my parents and her parents,' says Kabir. 'So, it is difficult to meet anybody else. There are some friends that I've not met for some six years. They keep trying to contact me but I'm always like, "I'm in a meeting; I'll call you back."'

Many men who were forced to work from home during the pandemic found themselves in a position to take on more responsibilities at home. Some tried to learn to cook, some did more cleaning and most spent more time with their children. And as offices open and encourage them to return, they might be eager to escape the household chores, but they would like to remain engaged and involved with their children. Both men and women would like to return to the office on a few days at least as they miss personal interactions with their bosses and colleagues, which they feel are important to their work.

Ravi and Sonali have friends amongst their colleagues but maintain a professional distance. 'We discuss the boss, deadlines, work pressure, less salary—wherever you go, that is very common,' says Sonali. 'But they will not tell you the true things. They will put you down. They are your competition. We also complain but we are also their competition.'

Gopal says, 'I would say that you have to be diplomatic. If you are diplomatic, you can do anything. I will not say, be honest in the office. I don't recommend anyone to be honest at office, I never recommend anyone to be dishonest at office, I say be diplomatic. A diplomatic person knows what to share and what not to share.'

The sense of loneliness and isolation that we pick up in our conversations with Gopal, Krish and Samar appears to be missing in their married peers. A spouse may provide the support and companionship that is missed from the distancing of non-work friends and the frenemy-style relationships at work. Or, maybe, marriage makes one more open to understanding others and accepting compromises. Marriage also appears to slow down the sprint and enforce a pacing that may work out well for the career marathon. The respondents who are actually trying to juggle their priorities seem to be more confident of finding their balance than the ones who are only worrying about how it might slow them down.

'Moving from the initial to mid-level rungs of the corporate ladder brings its own transitional stress. Just like with any other transition, our expectations play a central role in how we handle it,' says Kalyani Capoor. 'The grass often seems greener on the other side of the fence only and precisely because it's on the other side. The more realistic these expectations are, the smoother the transition. Promotions bring with them new sets of demands. Suddenly from being one of them, you are now the one. Honest personal equations at work seem to become even fewer and added responsibilities make it even more difficult to nurture meaningful friendships outside of it. Having a steady partner with whom you share a healthy and close bond can act as a great de-stressor at this mid-level transition.'

At this mid-level stage too, the perception seems to be that the next level will be better. Hetal says, 'We can get the work done instead of doing it ourselves. I won't have to work more; I will be able to give time to my family. There will be flexibility at work.' The Quantum research report says, 'Employees rationalize the need to work harder by believing that this stage is one last layer of hardship before they finally get to progress to a more powerful role. While employees want quick/fast-tracked growth, they believe the hardships and challenges they go through would provide them an entry card to their desired success in the future.'

Cheryl says, 'There is nothing to do but cope up with the pressure because it is [present] every month. If I over-achieve this month, then my boss' expectations from me next month are more. So, the pressure is definitely going to increase . . . Only achieving my target won't be sufficient for me, the expectation will be to over-achieve. I don't want to fail.'

Kabir says, 'These days what happens is your boss starts expecting extra from you because he also faces that. It's like if you can do this, then you can do even more.'

There is a certain level of competence and confidence that comes with the progress made so far. And the desire for more appears sharper. This also seems to be the time to evaluate and adjust career and life goals. Am I really doing well, especially in comparison with my peers? If I am, how do I stay ahead? If I'm not, what can I do to fix it and make up for it? Career progress is a critical parameter for validation of success but it is not the only dimension. Changing a job can be seen as an easy way to fix the problem that has been identified.

'Sudden realization of poor health, mental and emotional burnout, the prospect of marriage, having children, lack of time for family and friends and its overall negative impact on one's well-being operate as external factors that force the employee to rethink their current lifestyle and priorities,' says Quantum's research report. 'As employees reach the tipping point, the chances of attrition go up significantly.'

Ashok Capoor says, 'One of the most difficult transitions is from being a fresher to entering middle management, where you are supposed to manage a team. The skill set required for doing your job as an individual is very different from that required for managing a team. My experience has shown that freshers who are extremely good performers sometimes fail miserably when they have to manage a team. Middle management is most vulnerable as the growth prospects become limited and there is also pressure to perform in a certain manner, as your juniors wait ready to replace you.'

Corporate employees at the mid-level start to notice that there are fewer roles tending towards senior management and they see the number of promotions amongst their peer group shrinking as they approach it. They also face the double threat of seniors who may fiercely hold on to their positions for longer and more skilled juniors who may climb the hierarchy faster.

R.R. Nair says, 'The organizational structure is shifting shape from the traditional pyramid to a more concave shape, which is squeezed in the middle. This is a direct consequence of cost pressures and automation. Large batches of freshers are being hired for their digital skills and senior expertise is required to navigate the dynamic shifts we are seeing in the business environment. The contribution at the mid-level is being questioned, adding to the role stress and threatening the work identity. There is a conflict of interest between career goals, mid-level challenges and organizational costs.'

The respondents we have met seem particularly sensitive about not getting a promotion that they feel they rightfully deserve and this is often the real catalyst for moving jobs. Not moving up the corporate ladders fast enough appears to be perceived as a failure.

Jai moved jobs from an Indian bank to a global bank. He says, 'It is for growth. You want to come out of your routine because sometimes the work becomes monotonous and you want to try new things. That is why you jump jobs. In my last company, I had issues with the bosses. I was doing well but I didn't get a promotion, which really hurt. Someone comes from outside and they have a soft corner for him and you don't get the promotion. That is why I took the call.'

'I was meeting my targets and there was a colleague of mine who was not doing good work but had a good relationship with our boss and he got a promotion, but I did not,' says Onkar. 'So that is the political side of this corporate world. You should be on good terms with your manager. Then you will get promoted and hard work does not matter so much. I feel a little cheated and bad as well. I gave everything for the company and at the last someone else got the promotion. Somehow that demotivates you.'

'Managing your boss is important in the corporate world and definitely bears a role in career growth, whether we like it or not. If your boss likes you, this will help your career in a lot of subtle ways,' says Ashok Capoor. Respondents who claim to have a comfortable equation with their bosses also show less urgency to leave their jobs for better prospects.

Cheryl says, 'I would definitely like to move on. But right now, it is not the time. If I go into a new job, again there will be new challenges. I would like to plan my family here, settle down and then maybe, I can look for another option, when I am ready to accept the new challenges.'

'I have not changed [jobs] because I have got lots of opportunities here; my bosses are good,' says Ravi. 'Actually it is the salary which gives me mental peace. My work timings are very flexible. So, I have no problems. I can come early if Sonali is working late. Suppose if I am late, she can come early.'

Keeping track of opportunities is not always to get a new job. As Sonali explains, 'Here it is very common every month or two, to get an opening through LinkedIn or from any HR consultant. It is fine to go for an interview and see what they are offering, just to see what is available and what the market rates are. If we do not explore, we will not come to know. We should be able to tell our manager at times, during appreciation or promotion or during appraisal. "Boss, this is what is going on in the market. If you are giving [equal incentives], then, yes; otherwise, no. I have other opportunities."' Gopal says, 'Right now, we have plenty of sources for information like Glassdoor, where people give reviews about their companies. We can get an idea from there.'

Their relationship with the boss seems to be top of mind for most of the respondents. Jai feels there are too many layers of approvals required for every decision. He says, 'We have to wait till the ultimate top boss gives his decision. It takes a certain amount of time and because of that, our work gets delayed. Till we don't get the approval, we cannot execute our work.'

Anvi says, 'We cannot back-answer the boss. Whether we are right or wrong, we have to listen to the boss.' Ravi says, 'It is very common but here [India] having a good rapport with the boss is more important than your work. Work may not appreciated but your rapport with the boss is appreciated.' Gopal says, 'You cannot be sentimental in professional life. Once, I had made a mistake and my manager came to defend me. If I had not made that mistake then I might not have seen that either.'

Staying on the right side of the boss seems to be a primary concern at this mid-career level, also because respondents are more confident of gauging and testing the relationship now that they have some experience. Many respondents had stories of how they and their fellow team members would bond and help each other in figuring out the right moment to approach the boss for approvals they needed. Informal WhatsApp groups of the team and direct conversations with those few people who are considered more knowing are mentioned.

'We have seen informal peer group support increasing over the last five to six years, as a lot of dilemmas are common, and sharing with someone who is in a similar situation is more comfortable,' says R.R. Nair, 'Despite company resources like anonymous hotlines, there is a significant reticence with sharing problems with strangers, a sort of disclosure discomfort. The COVID pandemic has eased this slightly because it is a widely shared threat and works as an external hook to anchor and discuss their individual issues.'

The mid-level respondents are also bosses themselves but few of them are aware of how they might come across to those who report to them. There is an underlying implication that either they are more reasonable and sensitive leaders or that they do not have as much room for manoeuvring as their own bosses have. 'I am very good with my team, but there are times when I have to get angry with them,' says Cheryl. 'Sometimes I don't talk to them properly. I demand that "this has to be done today; I don't know how you are going to do it, but you have to." These are *my* words, true, but I am also under a lot of pressure. So, sometimes, I do misbehave.'

Gopal says, 'I have been working for eight years. When I see a new recruit, I see my reflection in that person. I was like that person. I used to think that I was a king, and I didn't respect seniors. Now I try to explain to him that I used to be like him too.'

The mid-career stage coincides with the mid-life stage and work would also have a prominent role in any crisis of the self. The aspirations, vulnerabilities and insecurities of the corporate world have about as much impact on personal lives as individual aspirations, vulnerabilities and insecurities would on career journeys. The same applies to both life and work experiences and their lessons. Many of our respondents use corporate jargon to refer to their personal lives, talking of alignment of their key performance measures or winning approval from their spouses. They wield their corporate persona in wider social interactions too, and corporate designations, as we already know, determine status in personal networks as well. It is not absolute success but our relative standards of success that make us feel like we are winning or losing in the game.

Gopal says, 'I see people who go through a lot of struggle, and they are not able to have any connection. But they want to be happy, and they try to be happy. They stay positive; it is about mentality and people go through struggle every day. I have also struggled a lot. I am not going to do this job till eternity. I want to start something of my own, but till the time I am able to do it, I will go with the flow.'

'Corporate people will be more focused,' says Cheryl, 'because, you know, they must [be driven] in order to gain something. They have a sense of, maybe you call it, style or, you call it, behaviour. So, they will only follow those things.'

Our corporate careers and lives have the span of a marathon, but our status-consciousness, competitiveness and impatience often drive us to view them as a collection of shorter sprints.

I know from my own experience that most of us don't pace ourselves very well because there is always some prize in sight and we like to believe that once we have it, we'll be satisfied, but then the next milestone becomes visible, and we keep racing towards it.

13

Shifting Goals

Climbing up the rungs of the corporate ladder leads us to senior management levels, and it appears that being at the top of the status hierarchy is worth the effort and sacrifices it takes to get us there. 'Those in a position of power are able to best utilize the benefits and perks offered by an organization,' says Quantum's research report. 'Flexible work hours/workplace, leave policies, holidays etc., are easier for them to avail than those at a junior position. In fact, currently there is a stigma associated with employees of a junior position availing these benefits, as they are often not trusted to use them diligently and ethically. Therefore, availing these benefits come with a certain flexibility stigma. As one moves higher up the ladder, this stigma disappears as people are expected not to question the decisions made by senior management.'

Varun, who heads the finance function in an Indian company, says, 'You have to understand what your priorities are, both on the personal and the professional front. At this stage of your career, the personal one takes a bigger priority compared to the professional one, so understanding the priorities at the right age and the right stage is important.'

Varun and his wife, Preeti, who works in project management with a multinational company, have had an interesting journey on their way to the top of their careers. They currently live in their apartment in one of the luxury properties in Gurugram and enjoy all the perks of the corporate lifestyle but getting here has not been easy. Both of them have worked in different companies and shifted many jobs for a variety of personal and professional reasons.

When their teenage son was much younger, he had health issues that kept him in and out of hospitals for a couple of years. Preeti, as mentioned in Chapter 3, chose to prioritize their son over her career and Varun supported her in this as much as he could. Both of them are grateful for the flexibility and support of their bosses and colleagues at the time, but they also recall how hard they had to work to meet their professional commitments. 'My colleagues and my seniors knew about it, and they were supportive as long as the job was getting done,' says Varun. 'In short, the job was getting done right. Even when he was in the hospital a couple of times, I used to be taking calls and I was working from there, although I was not in the office.'

Now that they are both in senior positions, Preeti and Varun feel they can make up for the sacrifice and struggles they went through in their early and mid-careers. Preeti says, 'Although Varun has done great in his career, for him his family comes first and he is always thinking about us, planning for a holiday or something. Even his future planning is family-oriented.' This stage seems to be the time to reap the rewards of the hard work of the past, to make up for lost family time, to indulge them with the luxuries that are now affordable, maybe in part to banish any sense of regret or guilt.

Preeti is also making up for lost time in her career. She and Varun have been consistently aligned in their priorities: in the early and mid-stages, Varun's career was their priority and now it is her career, though, it doesn't translate into her giving up her family responsibilities. It helps that both of them are in senior enough roles to be able to demand rather than request flexibility.

'She is always very focused despite having a busy schedule,' says Varun. 'In fact, she is more busy than I am. Her work schedule is far more demanding than mine, but she still takes the time to make sure what kind of food I am getting and what other family members are getting. I am very particular about what I eat so she makes sure I have the right kind of food in the morning [and] for lunch and dinner. She also takes care of our son and everything. She is very focused despite being very busy anytime of the day. I might tell her I want something, and she will ensure that it is available.'

Karan, a general manager with an Indian company in Bombay, prefers not to avail so much of the flexibility that is available to him. He says, 'At the top level, the expectations are only about results. Nobody wants to understand what kind of efforts you are putting if the results do not come.'

His journey has been very different from Preeti and Varun's. A successful graduate of his company's fast-track programme, Karan is younger than most of his peers. His wife, Diya, has given up her senior position in the hospitality industry to start her career again in the education sector. Now that she has more personal time, they are planning to have a child. Karan's mother, who lives with them, manages the home and household work with minimal help from them. There is not much need for flexibility as yet and Karan feels no compunctions about keeping his focus firmly on his career for now.

Shyam's profile seems similar to that of Karan's on paper. He is also a general manager at a consulting company in Bangalore and lives with his wife and mother. Unlike Karan, he seems to be trying to feel a little detachment from his career and work. It's not difficult to understand where this comes from when we consider his experience of being laid off at a crucial point in his career and life, as mentioned in chapters 5 and 6. The trauma has not yet faded. He says, 'When I didn't have a job, at that time, I didn't have many options. The more loyal you are to the organization, the more it will hurt. If you cry for the food, only then you get the food. You have to have the potential to be pulled out by other organizations. At the senior level, there are people out there who will be waiting to pull you down. Because at work, nobody belongs to anyone, they are just there to work.'

The corporate persona, which the freshers struggle to develop and mid-career professionals become less conscious about, seems less like something put on and more like second skin at this stage. There is little dissonance reported between their professional and personal avatars, and much less venting. A probable reason could be that at this level asserting oneself is not just permissible but expected as part of the role. So, there would not be much that they feel they cannot express at work. Another reason could also be that they have had years to practice, fine-tune and perfect their professional persona, so it feels much more comfortable by now.

The respondents in this cohort talk much more confidently and seem totally convinced in the rightness of their views. They exude an air of authority despite the interviews being held in their homes and outside of their working hours. The respondents from other cohorts speak with less certainty and seem to say similar things, and they have common experiences. The attitudes and experiences at the senior level appear more individual and unique. There is a sense of isolation, and they seem to feel little need to conform or to consider other perspectives.

Robert Sutton, management specialist, professor and author, said in an interview with McKinsey Quarterly in 2009, 'When people are in positions of power, for better or worse, they often become sort of oblivious to the needs and actions of the people who have less power than them.' This appears to hold true for our senior respondents, despite their own experiences at the lower levels of the corporate hierarchy, which are still fresh in their minds. They profess some sympathy for their subordinates but also appear to see them as disconnected from their own past selves in the same stages.

'They want to know each and everything, like why they are being told to do something,' says Karan. 'When we were freshers, we used to do what we were told. We never used to argue but they will, like if it is a weekend then they will say, "sorry, I can't work, it is the weekend. I will do the work on Monday." I hear from friends, and they will say, "the fresher behaved in a bad manner but we never [behaved] like this."'

Diya recalls a candid conversation she had with her friend. 'The young generation gets offended easily and if you ask someone for a glass of water, they will take it on their ego,' she says. 'I was talking to my friend in one of the event management companies and she told me that during her recruitment interviews, she asks the candidates to close the doors and fetch a glass of water. She says that if the person is not comfortable and their body language is not proper, she rejects them. "My event management company will succeed when the employees are ready to do anything for the client. They shouldn't have an ego," she told me.'

'At the senior level, people have some discretionary indulgence,' says R.R. Nair. 'There are some decisions that are entirely at their discretion, and it is easy to slip into being unmindful of the concerns of others. Exceptional leaders understand the value of socialized power, which comes from making the people on their teams feel equally powerful, valued and respected. Every company would have some unmindful leaders who become consumed by their power and their need to be centre stage to shape the course of events. They easily become oblivious to the needs of lesser mortals.'

'Seniority in the corporate context brings with it a complex mix of power and responsibility,' says Kalyani Capoor. 'You are the boss, and the buck stops with you. You are the face of the organization and the arc lights rarely dim. You have achieved the ultimate milestone and are expected to have all the answers. The perks and privileges at this stage of course are many and magnificent not the least of which is power. And power is a double-edged sword and what that sword does depends solely on the hand that holds it. This sword is in fact the most effective in the hands of a leader who needs it the least to boost his worth.'

Elevated status allows for a new assertiveness that is not easily challenged by those lower in the hierarchy, and this assertiveness is often used to correct the personal–professional balance for oneself. Finding oneself on the other side of the 'boss dynamic' is empowering and also adds a new pressure of matching up to the projected image. One side effect of this may be the difficulty in showing vulnerability—the respondents tended to gloss over any insecurity and many of the 'bad boss' stories we heard across the cohorts appear to be the repercussions of repressing personal inadequacies rather than addressing them.

Tanya, sales head for a large company, says, 'Some senior people, like a client of mine, tend to lead from the ego. It's transparent to everyone but him. He will call for a meeting and then make everyone wait for a long time. During a discussion, he will take exception to one stray comment and get defensive and angry. He may take his time to arrive at a decision or insist on more meetings even when there is no new information. I may be at the same level of seniority but I can't let my ego get involved too and jeopardize the deal. I have to be patient.'

Shyam says, 'If you are not dominant, it won't help you. I have people in my team who are submissive. I tell them, "You can't be a manager and you won't progress in your career."'

'Leaders are often lonely,' says Kalyani Capoor. 'The role demands a persona of invulnerability. If the designation starts defining the person, this persona is likely to extend to connections outside of work as well. This doesn't then allow them to be authentic. Not allowing oneself to express any vulnerability is unhealthy enough. What can truly compound it further is when you don't even allow yourself to get in touch with it. "I can't be vulnerable" soon starts to become "I am not vulnerable" and the road is paved for severe stress and worse.'

'The need to constantly assert one's power and status also results in a highly masculine work environment,' says the Quantum research report. 'While the need is to balance both masculine and feminine styles of management, employees often gravitate towards an authoritarian and assertive work style, hence keeping the power distance alive.' Most women at this stage tend to subdue overt expressions of their femininity to fit in.

With many companies now actively seeking diversity at the senior level, the gender gap here appears to have a little more to do with availability of talent than bias. As mentioned in the previous chapter, many women tend to put their careers on hold when they have children, and quite a few do not return, whether by their own preference or because they are discouraged by the more obvious bias at the mid-level and the lack of support systems at work and/or at home. The few women respondents we met at this stage either have no children or their children are almost grown-up, like in Preeti's case.

Shyam believes that the reputations that corporations build about themselves are not quite accurate, and the glamour that is seen from the outside is often just a projection. 'There is a corporate myth,' he says. 'You see something different from outside and when you go inside, it's different. In a consulting organisation, for the outside world we may see this company is set at this level [of corporate image]. There may be a certain respect for whatever the subdivision is. So, when a person joins there, they may feel "my life is going to be like this." But when they get inside the organisation, their life will be totally different. And second are the fancy titles you see in an organisation. The myth that you develop outside is that okay, a title of a vice president means you'll get perks, you'll get a company card, etc. You'll see all these fancy things but when you get inside, you may feel that it is just a title.'

He is more cynical than the other respondents but also very confident that he understands the corporate game well. Shyam uses his experience and learning to build his approach to team building. 'If they feel engaged, then they will deliver their hundred per cent,' he says. 'If they are disconnected and they don't understand anything, then they won't give their hundred per cent. If it is only work, work, work, and there are no activities for learning anything beyond work, they will find it monotonous. I make sure I work with my HR team and give them training-like activities to make them feel like a family. Normally, we spend more time in a corporate office than at home. So, if they don't feel a sense of belonging here, then they won't work with . . . full focus.'

While the other cohorts appear to look forward to company activities and events as a break or some sort of reward, the senior people see them as part of their work, necessary to build team bonding and a sense of belonging. It takes a lot of coordination and planning to organize these events, probably even more when they have to be done virtually since the pandemic increased travel risks. Coordinating time, especially with global teams, and ensuring participant engagement on a video conference is a big challenge and not so easily outsourced to event management vendors.

Ritu, a senior manager at a global technology company, recalls being 'voluntold' to a team to plan and manage a recent team event. I haven't heard the word before, so she explains that 'voluntold' is when your boss assigns to you projects and activities that were meant to be voluntary but attracted too little enthusiasm from actual volunteers. 'When your boss tells you to take on a project that's not directly related to your job description, what can you say,' says Ritu. 'They make it sound like you have a choice, but actually it is added pressure since the request has come directly from your manager. You put additional pressure on yourself, thinking that if you say no, the boss might think that you aren't a team player and there is also fear of possible repercussions later, especially during performance reviews. However sometimes this push has helped too, as it makes me learn something new.'

The rise of technology and use of computers have eliminated many secretarial and administrative positions. More than a decade ago, a senior management position came with the perk of having a secretary/assistant who organized the schedule for the boss and did all the coordination and administrative work like filing expense reports and booking travel. Now there are smaller administrative departments that cater to multiple managers, and the expectation is that the managers handle most of the scheduling, coordination and other administrative tasks themselves with the help of digital platforms. Some senior people struggle to adapt to the technological skills required and try to delegate these tasks to their juniors.

The Quantum research points out that presently the senior level is about transitioning from the cultural code of hard work to smart work, freeing up time for reflection on business needs and personal life. The report says, 'While constant delegation is also considered a sign of laziness by some, most believe it is the smartest way of getting jobs done. Some managers also believe delegation is one of their methods of training employees for more challenging roles.'

I remember feeling a little uncomfortable when I first transitioned to a senior management role. Suddenly, there seemed to be a lot more value attached to my time and effort. I was accustomed to doing my own paperwork and taking care of personal errands but now, even in the informal environment of advertising, I was expected to delegate some of my work. Since I disliked doing these monotonous tasks, I should have been happy to pass them along, but I felt a little guilty about it because I knew how demotivated I had felt when my bosses had done the same to me.

I did enjoy the respect that came with my new status, but I also felt like it was cutting me off from a sense of comfort and belonging within the work group. I found that many of the people who had previously talked to me quite candidly were becoming more guarded. Some of them became overtly flattering and some of them became too reticent. And, of course, I struggled because I had subscribed so completely to the 'hard work' code that working in another way was inconceivable. I imagine quite a few people might find this a difficult adjustment but not many of the respondents were able to articulate it.

Ashok Capoor says, 'It is a myth that working hard is extremely important for growth in the organization. I feel results are the key ingredient for growth and that can easily be achieved through smart work, i.e., delegating work which is less important to juniors. In my life, I have had to hardly ever work beyond the eight hours in office. It is possible to have a healthy work–life balance. In fact, when you grow in your career, it is most important how you manage the work through your juniors. You should delegate and have some form of control. The team needs to feel you trust them and there has to be transparency in how you give feedback. At the very senior levels, you are bound to feel lonely and isolated because juniors feel that they must maintain a distance and respect for the position you occupy.'

'Leadership style also depends to some extent on follower tendencies,' says R.R. Nair. 'If the followers have a low tolerance for ambiguity and prefer to be submissive, then they respond better to a dominant leader. It is important for leaders to understand the key drivers and motivations of the people on their teams, including what types of experiences have shaped their attitudes, aspirations and values. They need to play the role of coaches and create enabling conditions for their teams to perform. It is vital for leaders to be prepared with the skills that can lead to team performance and growth.'

Karan and Diya admit to still feeling work pressures despite their years of experience, but they know the coping mechanisms that work for them. 'You have to handle it on your own,' Diya says. 'Your stress is your stress, and my stress is my stress. The thing is how you will handle it. For Karan, he says it is exercise. For me, it is being quiet and being by myself. I need my space. For you, handling stress might be different. Maybe you might want to talk to someone. For some people, it is just picking up the phone and talking to their parents while others talk to their friends.'

'Sometimes there is sacrifice [involved] at work also,' says Varun. 'There may be some exciting project going on, but saying no to it is also fine, because you know that you cannot handle it; whatever the reason, it could be your personal life or your professional life. Like I said, we have to be very assessing in our decisions. You can't be overestimating yourself and saying, "yes I can do this, and also that."'

The COVID-19 pandemic has added new layers of stress for senior leaders. Apart from the obvious challenges of managing and monitoring their teams virtually, they also have the pressure to respond sensitively to the crisis, to ensure that support is actually provided to their employees and vendors at the ground level as well as manage their own and their companies' image perceptions. Layoffs and cost cutting, however necessary they may seem, appear insensitive at such a time and add to professional insecurity and competition at all levels of the corporate hierarchy. Criticism can be personal, brutal and swift, thanks to social media.

In Chapter 7, I mentioned Praneel, a senior executive in the retail sector and a respondent in my Google Forms survey in September–October 2021, who tells us about business leadership reactions to the COVID-19 pandemic. He says, 'Mostly the reactions have been contextual. We did have to take some very difficult and harsh calls. We did make sure that we at the senior most level subject ourselves to tougher impact than the rest of the teams. But the sheer scale of impact and misery has made us—well, at least me—more aware of the financial and family context of our relatively junior colleagues.'

R.R. Nair says, 'Post COVID [lockdown], I am sensing a visible change in the way leaders tend to act and behave. They are becoming more mindful and sensitive, more enquiring about their subordinates' state of health and mind. There is more inclusivity, empathy and patience. They are realizing that it is crucial for them to be proactive in sensing and judging the moods and needs of the people reporting to them. The entry to a senior role is a passport issued by the organization, but the onus for responsibility is shifting to the individual. They need to develop the capacity to stay relevant. My clients are discovering hidden diamonds of leadership talent at the skip levels.'

Senior colleagues are often expected to have things figured out, to be able to give answers rather than express self-doubt. This makes it even more difficult to admit mistakes, and, at this level, people seem to project more confidence than they actually feel. Some of it comes from the benefit of experience, some of it from having a stronger financial cushion and some from the elevated status and recognition. As the Quantum research report says, 'This new position of power is thoroughly enjoyed as with it comes immense respect and status, and employees now contribute towards keeping the corporate caste system alive.'

The status and success of seniors appear to strongly reinforce the codes of hard work and sacrifice at the lower levels of one's career, and this is what they continue to expect from their subordinates. It's a bit like the parental stories we have heard growing up, of how hard our parents had it when they were of our age, and now that the world is easier, they worry that we won't be as tough and resilient as them. There is a tendency amongst senior professionals to attribute all their career growth and success to the difficult parts of their journey since those stand out so starkly in their memory. So, if their subordinates may share their challenges, they may see them as opportunities for growth and be less empathic. It seems as if by the time we arrive at the position where it is possible to make real changes to our work culture, our desire to do so is fading.

A lot more leeway seems to be extended to one's boss rather than to one's subordinates at this stage too. Karan says, 'Many times I feel like things are too much, and I should probably give them back to my boss. Then I realize that if somebody is talking to you in a harsh tone, you have to empathize. You have to put yourself in their shoes and think about what they are going through. You have to think that it is something that is unavoidable for them. The biggest rule that I have made and that I have imparted to Diya as well is that you should never reply to an email when you are angry, no matter how harsh or angry the message you have received. Otherwise, you tend to say things that you do not mean. Always take an hour's breather and then think about what you could [say].'

Sudhir is the CEO of the India office of a well-funded global start-up. He has a very friendly personality and is easy to talk to. So, his friends, family and colleagues naturally tend to seek him out for career advice and mentoring. He says, 'People tend to get nervous whenever there is a change in the company's management or when they get a new boss. They worry that they won't be able to build a good rapport or that they will not be able to adjust to the changes that will surely come. When a new boss arrives, he/she tends to make all the right noises before they start to shake things up. I advise people not to self-sabotage. Just be friendly and agreeable to the boss' overtures. If you are uncomfortable, you can start looking for a new job but there's no point in rocking the boat right from the start by being uncooperative or disagreeable.' In the constant attempt to avoid offending a boss, it is possible that real and relevant information, feedback and ideas may also be lost.

It occurs to me that reaching the top and getting ahead of the game may be a good moment to take a pause, to enjoy the view and reflect on one's journey. Our respondents, however, seem compelled to keep looking forward and working towards their next goal, whether short term or long term. 'Important career decisions and plans such as long-term travel, relocation, job changes etc., are carefully evaluated keeping one's family in mind,' says the Quantum report. 'Their senior position also allows them to be assertive and put their needs first without much worry, as their seniority and expertise is always in demand.'

'Five years is a good [period of] time to stay in a company,' says Shyam. 'After that, your growth stops. Then more than an asset, you will be a liability to the company and eventually [be] replaced by someone who will do your work for a lower salary. You have to take care of your children and have good financial support as well. I think everything is about balance. One side is you forget your family and only think about your profession, that is not good. If you think only of your family and not about your profession, that's also not good.'

'Generally people would like to retire by the age of sixty, but I probably want to retire by the age of fifty five,' says Karan. 'I feel that I should be able to generate enough funds in my life with ownership of about six to seven properties—enough money so that I can live the rest of my life with her peacefully, and we can endlessly roam around the world. You know, just explore the world that we are in and lead a kind of nomadic life.' Diya says, 'In my childhood we used to visit Goa and we would see these old couples there, who came to the hotels and resorts. They and the foreign tourists would be just [whiling away time] for a couple of months. After we retire, why should we not also enjoy life like that?' I find it interesting that it's Karan, who refuses to avail of the flexibility he is entitled to, who sees retirement as a break, while the others who are finding more balance in their lives are not aiming for such an escape.

Saving for retirement starts early in India, almost from the very start of a job as most companies offer salaries along with retirement and tax saving benefits, like contributions to the provident fund. Yet, retirement itself seems very far and there are more immediate goals to focus on. It's only when we reach the senior levels, where there is more financial security and we can start to see our retirement on the horizon, that we start making more concrete plans.

Achieving the high status and lifestyle we had aspired to, along with the support systems and expertise we have developed and earned, feels good but is not quite enough to slow us down. We keep moving forward. It seems as if our career evolution cannot overcome our deep-seated cultural conditioning. We continue to look up and ahead in reverence and work our way towards the next milestone, even if that now skews more personal than professional.

14

Seeking Relevance

With the increasing life spans of affluent Indians and the advances in nutrition and healthcare, sixty or sixty-five as the age of retirement doesn't make much sense anymore. The premature onset of lifestyle diseases and conditions brings an unexpected advantage to senior citizens. A forty-year-old may have similar health conditions as that of a sixty-year-old, with only half the work experience, and this person will probably learn how to manage these conditions better by the time he/she reaches sixty. While many companies have yet to change their retirement policies officially, quite a few of them are willing to give extensions to valued leaders, particularly when they have a credible standing with critical investors, industry forums, media platforms and customers. Quite often, they re-hire some of their retired employees on a contractual basis in advisory positions.

'Today few people at a senior level retire at sixty,' says Raja, who chose to retire from his position as chief operating officer of a prominent Indian business group. 'So people look at me with a mix of curiosity, scepticism and respect.'

In the retired cohort, Raja is also one of the few respondents who chose to move away from the big cities to a hill station in Tamil Nadu. Only five of the thirty-six respondents to my survey on Google Forms currently reside in small towns.

The rest of them continue to live in big cities where corporate businesses have their headquarters, with the majority of them living in Bombay. Perhaps, it is due to this skew that only three of the respondents no longer work in any capacity, four of them work without pay and the rest of them are engaged in paid work primarily, in addition to some unpaid work.

Eight of the respondents are seventy-one years old, or older, and the rest of them are between sixty and seventy years old. Given the gender gap at the senior level, it is no surprise that only four of the respondents are women. There is no notable difference in the responses of the women and the men at this stage, probably because all of them are comfortable financially and most family responsibilities have already shifted or are in the process of shifting to the next generation.

Jayant is in his early sixties and lives in the Delhi–NCR area. He retired as senior partner of a global executive search firm, and he currently has a few paid positions as an independent director on company boards, and he also works for a few non-governmental organizations without any remuneration. He says, 'In India, people feel sorry for you when you mention that you are retired. It is still seen as a taboo.' This seems strange given that Jayant and the rest of the respondents are all highly functioning, active and influential people—a far cry from the outdated, Bollywood-stereotype retirees shown as declining, ailing elders who are a drain on family resources. I think the taboo may not be about being retired per se but more to do with the unwelcome perceptions of being *vella* (colloquialism for doing nothing useful).

When both my grandfathers retired in the 1990s, one of them from the army and the other from the Indian Civil Service, they didn't continue to work but they remained busy. The former kept up his exercise regimen and got involved in his building's residents' society; the latter indulged in his reading habit and continued to participate in bridge tournaments. Both kept up with the news and regularly visited their clubs to play golf and to socialize. They enjoyed their retirement not as leisure but as time well spent. I remember their bafflement when my sister and I wanted to sleep or watch television on vacations when we visited them. Wasting time in this way was incomprehensible to them, as I am sure it still would be for many parents and grandparents.

Our cultural codes of hard work, sacrifice and competitiveness apply not just to jobs and careers but also to anything else we may choose to do, whether it is looking after a home, other family responsibilities or even our interests and hobbies. The respondents who are still working full-time in the corporate sector say they have little to no time to keep up with their hobbies and interests regularly. Most of their time is spent at work and whatever remaining time they have is mainly spent with family and a little with friends. Their vacations are mostly for travel or family events and emergencies, so it may be likely that by the time they retire, they may find it difficult to reconnect with their hobbies.

Busyness has gained acceptance as a status symbol across age groups. This is an insight from when I was working for some of the leading apparel brands in India. I feel it's also the reason why we feel compelled to share and compare our version of war stories, as mentioned in Chapter 2. Vacations are good for bragging rights, but they can only last so long and they don't bring us quite the same sort of admiration, especially when the level of busyness is presumed to equate to one's level of importance and influence amongst one's peers. Our family dynamics tend to revolve around individual states of busyness of all the members of the family. When one or more members of the family find themselves with more time on their hands, they may risk disrupting the balance.

The respondents of this generation of corporate professionals are skewed towards men, very few of whom have wives with equally busy careers. Their family dynamic was built on the husband being away at work and the wife running the home and family. While the wife and/or children may have at some point resented this, they have adapted. The husband and father may be carrying some residual guilt but he has already set the tone as being busy and he knows his children have their own careers and lives, and his wife her own work and interests. There is little other option for agreeable company if, as we see in this research sample, most of their friends and peers are still working. Finding other ways and means of staying busy is the smart thing to do.

R.R. Nair says, 'Redirected might be a better way of phrasing it as there is not a conventional sense of retiring today. This stage is about reinventing oneself to remain relevant, not just from a professional sense but also with regard to a dimension of well-being.'

The respondents who continue to work do so in an advisory, consulting or mentoring capacity. They offer strategic advice and guidance in their areas of expertise and experience but seldom have any operational responsibilities. Many of them work with organizations that are quite different from the ones they retired from, either in structure or scale or even sectors. While some of them claim to miss the direct impact and influence they used to wield, most of them say they enjoy the challenge of applying their skills to new sectors, of learning latest advances in technology and of teaching or mentoring the next generation of leaders.

Kalyani Capoor says, 'Since by this stage of life the lower needs on the hierarchy are mostly met, meaning and purpose often become the driving forces. And now there is the freedom to pursue these through voluntary work and mentoring. This freedom has been well and hard earned and therefore can be put to good use, thanks to the decades of rich experience that the mainstream corporate career has offered.'

'Currently retirement from jobs is not retirement in the real sense, as people sixty years and older are in great demand for advisory roles and on company boards,' says Ashok Capoor. 'It's a win-win situation. Companies benefit from their vast experience while they get to feel valued and productive. At this stage, money is not so critical so they continue to work, albeit less but with no stress. They have complete freedom to schedule their time, compensation and pace however they may choose.'

Financial considerations certainly do not seem to be quite as critical motivators at this stage as they are in the earlier stages of one's career. Like Jayant, quite a few of the respondents work for free in the social sector, whether with non-governmental, medical or educational organisations. This kind of work seems to be a source of tremendous satisfaction, articulated as a 'giving back' to society. They appear to feel an eagerness to be busy, to be perceived as relevant and valued contributors in whatever they do.

'There is maximum satisfaction in engaging with social causes now,' says R.R. Nair. 'Giving back is an important aspect of our way of life but normal full time corporate life doesn't allow for a direct experience of this beyond the mandatory CSR activities. There is a spiritual realization of wanting to be caring and supportive, to increase the feeling of belonging in the community and contributing towards the harmony we want to be part of. Perhaps, there might also be a certain sense of guilt for the societal privileges we have been granted. Since we have done very well for ourselves, we want to contribute to good causes, and we can do that by leveraging our managerial and leadership skills as well as our corporate networks. The internal satisfaction here is more implicit; the privilege of serving is very motivating and fosters a sense of collective pride rather than individual pride.'

For some respondents, the transition to an advisory role has been more seamless since their last roles were also in an oversight or mentoring capacity, like chairman of the board or a CXO position. The others who had more operational roles and responsibilities have had to make some adjustments.

Balaraman spent thirty-four years in one global consumer goods company and retired after heading several of its business functions. He says, 'Moving away from being a manager to an advisor, [I realize that] the roles are different, and my leadership style has adapted to the new avatar.' 'At the core, my leadership style has not changed,' says Ambika, who retired as managing director of a prominent Indian consumer goods company. 'The context has changed and therefore, what is relevant to be effective has changed too.'

Though I didn't meet any of the retired respondents in person, I saw clear differences between them and the other cohorts. The officially retired professionals seem to exude a sense of calm, patience and approachability though they may be just as busy. They lack the overwhelming sense of urgency and pressure that the other cohorts display when discussing their careers. Perhaps, it's because their significant milestones have already been achieved. Their current work and accomplishments seem important and meaningful but not essential to their sense of worth, which also appears to be more secure and robust at this stage. I sense a vibe of 'been there, done that' behind their quiet confidence and their imperviousness to the stress that the other cohorts display.

There are mixed feelings reported on the change in status that comes with retirement. It appears to be felt more intensely in the initial period after retirement, with more respondents in their early sixties mentioning this change as compared to the older respondents, who have had more time to adjust their expectations as well as re-establish their credentials as independent professionals.

Jayant says, 'I have realized that there are professionals who wanted to be very friendly with me while I was employed only because of my designation and influence.' 'Yes, certainly. The lack of official status, the designation and calling card, you can feel people finding you less "useful" in a so politely respectful way,' says Raja.

'No change is noticed,' says Biju, who used to head the finance team for one of the global agency networks and continues to offer financial guidance to a variety of organizations across sectors. He says, 'There is a marked increase in the respect given to my suggestions, opinions and advice. The culture in India of respecting elders still prevails.'

Nitin was chairman of a global infrastructure company before he retired and chose to stay on in Bombay so he could continue to be busy as an independent director on some boards, consulting on social projects and participating in industry forums. He says, 'There is no change on the personal level or with friends. The social level changes where invites are based on the position you occupy, and official socializing does decline.'

The corporate persona now seems indistinguishable from the personality and appears to be more authentic, open and accepting. 'Earlier people used to relate to me on the basis of the "position" I had and my "title". Now, it is for the value I bring as an individual, based on my experience, of course,' says Ambika. 'I get more regard, possibly due to my knowledge, skill and long experience,' says Harsh, who used to be a senior vice president and technical head for a global consumer goods company.

Thirty out of the thirty-six respondents say they do not want to return to their last official position even if it were possible. Only three say they would, and the rest are unsure.

The respondents say they enjoy the autonomy and flexibility of their present situations. They get to decide which projects, companies and sectors interest them and how much time they would like to invest in each of them. Since they have their savings secure and their children are independent, they also have the freedom to vary their professional charges for low-budget work that excites or challenges them. Most of them give their time and energy in return for little or no money to projects and causes close to their hearts, just for the chance to make an impact and experience the good feelings and gain the goodwill that follows.

Ambika says the greatest benefit of her current situation is the 'full freedom to spend my time the way I want to.' For Nitin, the lure is, 'the independence and the opportunity to work across a larger canvas, working for the underprivileged and contributing to the overall good of the country.'

There are some things they do miss from their previous roles as leaders in big corporations, like the opportunity to influence and direct the business vision and the camaraderie and networking with diverse people. Yet, most of them seem reluctant to give up the freedom they have now. It is the little things that sometimes frustrate them.

When asked what he misses, Balaraman says, 'Honestly nothing when looked at in hindsight. New opportunities gave me new dimensions and understanding of new areas, which were all quite exciting. I am putting all the learning of the previous thirty-four years to different use.'

'I miss the secretarial and administrative support that corporates provide,' says Nitin. The older respondents like Nitin have had secretaries or executive assistants for the last decade or more of their careers, so they did not learn the technological skills that younger generations would have picked up. It's doubly challenging to adapt to doing these tasks themselves as well as learning the technology that's available to make it easier. Some of them have remained in touch with their erstwhile secretaries and assistants, who are also retired, and reach out for occasional help.

The COVID-19 pandemic has accelerated their need to be more comfortable with technology. They have had to adapt to Zoom and other video meeting platforms in a much shorter span of time than when they had to learn to use email and other relevant computer skills earlier. Online transactions and net banking are more challenging because the security features make them far less user-friendly and require significant agility for navigation. Many would still prefer to do these tasks in person if they could or delegate the work to a spouse, child or assistant, if they have the option.

For those respondents who are not used to working with computers, it is an additional strain. Zoom fatigue is reported as a widespread impact of remote working, and if this is affecting younger tech-savvy professionals, it probably has an even bigger impact on senior citizens. Ambika says, 'Not travelling is a big adjustment. The biggest shift is in how work gets done—all online and in endless hours in front of a screen.'

'Not being in the office hurts,' says Biju. 'We can know people and their reactions better when we look into their eyes. Body language has a lot to explain or reveal in its nuances.' Nitin says, 'I miss the informal and social interaction and communication that take place in physical meetings around the lunch table and during informal breaks, giving you the opportunity to clarify your remarks and pick up nonverbal cues and signals. Creating private space at the residence for [virtual] meetings which go on throughout the day has required some adjustments.'

'Retirement brings with it its own transitional stress,' says Kalyani Capoor. 'Life as you knew it for almost four decades or so changes almost overnight. The problem rarely is that you miss the buzz and the busyness, the professional interactions or the secretarial support. While you do, these can be worked around. The real challenge is for the people who have identified themselves with their designation and whose brittle sense of self-worth was derived solely from it. This further gets compounded if the person has not adequately invested in hobbies or relationships.'

Most of the respondents display an eagerness and excitement to learn about the latest developments and update their own skill sets. As much as they enjoy mentoring younger people, they also claim to be willing to learn themselves. Harsh says, 'Despite the difficult times, I am able to utilize my time updating knowledge through webinars and personal contacts and also reading and writing scientific papers.'

'Continuous value addition keeps the treatment at a professional level,' says Balaraman. 'The moment you drop the ball and stop adding value, I think the perception will change,' he adds. The respondents are conscious of a fast-changing world where envisioning the future is becoming even more challenging. They want to stay relevant so they can continue to be productive and busy, so they are doing what they must to adapt.

The retired cohort has impressive experience and accomplishments behind them. Their status may not be quite as high as their previous designations but it is not too far below either. It gains momentum from keeping busy and making valuable contributions where they can. So, they invest their time and energy in multiple streams, unlike the focus on one that they had to maintain earlier. They feel appreciated and gratified even when they work for smaller companies and sectors or contribute outside the corporate domain towards social good. They display a renewed authenticity and new humility, now that they don't have the full force of a corporation behind them. There appears to be an underlying fear of becoming irrelevant or obsolete that drives them to keep up with the latest developments but not in the frenzied manner of younger professionals. They maintain a sense of balance and gravity that may come from knowing clearly what they can bring to an assignment and not being in a tearing hurry to get to their next one.

15

The Corporate Continuum

I have likened corporate careers to a game of snakes and ladders many times in this book, starting from Chapter 1, but unlike the actual game, in our careers, we don't have a rule book or any visibility of the game board. We do not even get to practice and play it several times until we get a win. We are playing blind, not able to distinguish the ladders from the snakes, and so are the other players. Our careers, just like our lives and our country, tend to be unpredictable and chaotic. Business organizations try to impose structure, linearity and predictability to their operations and we try to do the same to our careers.

In my attempt to map the big picture, I am conscious of these limitations, most specifically the limitation of linearity. As marketers and account planners, when we average and approximate the lives of a segment of people to build our consumer profile, we know that the person we portray doesn't actually exist. The profile helps us simplify and get into our consumers' perspective, to understand the context and compulsions of their lives, to see our products and services as they would, as a means to help them think or do or feel something that is important to them. This simplification is necessary because we cannot grasp the actual diversity and complexity of our consumers and their lives and still be able to make meaningful business decisions.

This research project has been intended from the start to find answers to help us understand the rules and see the game board more clearly. So, the researchers at Quantum and I imposed linearity in our selection of respondents when we defined the cohorts of people we would study. All of them represent a successful point on the ladders going up but none of them has made it to their current point unchallenged or unscathed. I have tried to be mindful of this in telling their stories.

At this point, I feel we must also consider the corporate employees whom we have left out of the research—those who have either abandoned the game at some point or are caught in a slide down the snake or are taking a pause to reconsider their next move. Neither they nor we know how or when they might resolve this and find themselves back on a ladder, just as those who are currently climbing up a ladder don't know when their luck might take a downturn. It is the nature of the game, and our cultural understanding of karma helps us comprehend, if not accept it wholeheartedly.

From a distance, corporate careers look like the most attractive destination. They hold the lure of status, sophistication and glamour and appeal to our competitive ambition. There are some who resist the lure outright for a sense of calling, choosing to enter sectors like the armed forces, the civil service, medicine, education and the arts, some of which may be in the midst of becoming more corporate but not to a large or complete extent as yet.

There are those who may enter the fringes of the corporate world but cannot proceed further due to lack of right kind of education, credentials and connections. These are the operational workers and support staff who work in the corporate sector but whose prospects are limited from the beginning with smaller ladders available for them to climb. They may cheer some of the actual contenders for a CXO spot from the sidelines and be carried a little ahead with their momentum. For them, participation in the corporate world is in itself a win; those who want more will probably hustle with some sort of side gig, which they hope might grow into a viable option. There are many small-scale operations like these that provide the corporate world with specialized services like transport, catering, typesetting, printing, production, and event management, etc. They remain under the radar of the start-up ecosystem unless and until they are able to scale up their operations. Many of these set-ups have been struggling through the COVID-19 pandemic and some have even scaled back their business or shut down.

Freshers, from more promising backgrounds, entering the mainstream corporate world, by desire, design or parental pressure, come in with high expectations. They want to prove their worth, learn and grow quickly. Their lack of experience and low status in the corporate hierarchy make them feel vulnerable and unsure. They look to their bosses and seniors for guidance and as potential role models. Their first experiences are critical in shaping their professional skills and corporate persona. If they encounter harsh, domineering bosses, they might choose to emulate them or they might choose to be different, depending on whether they perceive the organizational culture rewarding or punishing such behaviour. Finding a good mentor at this stage helps them to understand and adjust more quickly, giving them the confidence to be efficient and effective.

Life, though, is not just about being efficient and effective. Freshers feel this most keenly but have no power to demand the flexibility to pursue their exercise routines or spend time with friends and family or keep up with their interests and hobbies. They have the least autonomy to decide how and when to do their work. They are monitored when they come into the office and they feel compelled to stay as long as it takes to get their work done or till their bosses leave, whichever comes later. Their convenience is the last priority when it comes to setting work deadlines and meeting schedules. Although they are entitled to vacations and other benefits, they cannot easily insist on utilizing these privileges in the face of a disapproving boss. They know that they will need one to two years of experience before they can change jobs and/or functions. Their friends and social networks equip them with a lot of information on the different types of jobs, bosses and companies available to them, when they are ready or able to exercise their options. Depending on their personality and experiences so far, the freshers display different degrees of conformity and varying expressions of resentment or rebellion, but they get a consistent message from their bosses, parents and other authority figures, that submission, learning and adjustment is the way towards success in this phase.

The changes imposed by the COVID-19 pandemic might seem superficially in their favour, but they also make the challenges so much bigger. Working from home makes it harder to feel a sense of belonging, to connect with colleagues and peers. Anyone who has worked with a remote boss knows the difficulties of communication and coordination. How can one observe the people and culture of a company when their interactions are limited to phone calls, Zoom meetings and emails? And while it seems that there may be more spare time on their hands and some flexibility in spending that time, I have heard from several people across industries of the regulatory systems in place to monitor and control the actual time spent on work. Again, this is more closely enforced for those at the bottom of the hierarchy.

Some people drop out of the game at this point but to do so, they need to have concrete support from their families. Studying further to improve one's skills and prospects is one option to get a temporary reprieve from the corporate world. Getting married is another but it is an escape plan only available for women. In our culture, a man must have a steady source of income to be considered eligible but a woman may be encouraged to take a break or leave a job so she can better manage the personal transition. Many freshers might dream of starting their own businesses, where they get to call the shots, but this option is viable only for the lucky few with financial backing and the right connections. They know that unknown investors would hesitate to back founders with so little experience.

At the mid-level, employees have more confidence and are more comfortable in the corporate environment, but they find themselves juggling many professional and personal responsibilities. They could use more flexibility but are afraid of being judged for asking for more or even taking advantage of what is already on offer. When they have children, women have to take maternity leave, but the length is at their discretion, and some might prolong the break depending on their child-care support systems at home and/or at work. Many companies also offer paternity leave but my sense is that there is some hesitation among new fathers to take it and those who do hesitate to extend it. Given our cultural preference for the traditional family structure of nurturing, available mothers and provider fathers, women are more likely to risk the flexibility stigma than men. And in the absence of strong support systems at home and/or at work, some women drop out of the corporate game on a temporary or permanent basis at this time. The pandemic has increased the likelihood of female dropouts as women are more vulnerable to job losses and layoffs, as mentioned in Chapter 8.

Without clear physical boundaries between home and office in work-from-home (WFH) situations, there is no real escape from either of the responsibilities. It is challenging to carve out adequate space and set up electronic devices and network bandwidth for each member of the family to be able to do their work with a measure of privacy in homes that were never designed for such use. Those with children have the added burden of ensuring their children pay attention to their online classes and also have other activities to keep them engaged and occupied. While most fathers are helping out, the primary burden seems to rest on the mothers.

This phase has intense pressure as competition is not restricted to the peer set alone—there are seniors above as well as juniors below who could make their positions redundant, there is also the pressure of job loss from digitization, automation and cost cutting, as R.R. Nair pointed out in Chapter 12. Performance at work is critical for promotions, but many feel that sometimes subjective reasons come into play when they are denied a promotion. They know that even good performance cannot help in the face of mass layoffs, which often happen in companies from a macro perspective and tend to contribute towards a sense of separation and alienation from the organization. This insecurity reaffirms perceptions of the declining value of loyalty in the corporate game. If you slide down a snake, you are on your own, so most professionals keep a lookout for opportunities and if a good one shows up, many of them prefer to take their chances and venture out rather than stick around to find out if there is any truth to their fears.

There are high expectations to manage—those that come from their bosses, which they must drill down to their teams, and those that come from their own selves and their families. Health conditions from long working hours, poor eating and exercise habits, stress and sleep deprivation start to show up now and they must be managed in the interest of productivity and progress. All these factor into career decisions but are prioritized in order of importance or urgency after career goals and the ambition for higher status. At this level, most professionals are aware of their chances of success in the larger game, and they strategize to better their odds.

There are professionals who are more confident of their success. Many of them have developed their negotiation skills as a winning strategy. They have a more direct and problem-solving approach to any issue they may face, and they choose to adjust and align their own goals and expectations with those of their bosses, teams and families rather than feel overwhelmed by it all. These professionals are less hesitant to have difficult conversations and ask for help and support, and they can be assertive about what they want. They seem to have some maturity in coping with their emotions and this makes them more rational and objective in their approach to their careers.

For some, there is a sort of cynicism, or worse, a hard realization that this game is not in their favour. In that case, a choice must be made—to accept and continue with a more realistic definition of success or to drop out and find new careers and goals. Switching jobs, functions or sectors is common among professionals, and some may even decide to set up independently as freelancers, consultants or entrepreneurs now that they have years of experience behind them and also access to developing eco-systems for freelancers and start-ups. There is anecdotal evidence of professionals leaving corporate careers to experiment widely with work like organic farming, movie-making or stand-up comedy.

Those who have to stay or choose to stay entrenched in the corporate game feel a little lost or beaten and carry a sense of dissatisfaction and defeatism even if they don't express it overtly. Their own low levels of motivation may be contagious, especially for impressionable freshers, who may become targets for their venting and frustration. Without an option outside the game, their best chance is to get some guidance. The competition and politics make it difficult to be vulnerable and ask for help within the organization but professional and personal networks outside of it may be more approachable. Those with good personal relationships will have better support systems.

Burnout is a real possibility, but it is not discussed or recognised. It's another weakness that we would not like to admit. There are personal factors at play that are encouraged by the culture of insecurity, distrust and intense pressure. Our dislike and disdain for pacing ourselves or slowing down come in the way of any preventive or curative solutions as does our hesitation to be vulnerable and ask for help.

While considerable organizational support is often available, there are some barriers that prevent its widespread utilization. Internal wariness and caution and distrust of the company culture vary as per individual personalities and experiences. One common barrier is that the immediate boss is often the gatekeeper to such resources. The boss–employee relationship is considered critical and managed carefully, so there are concerns with personal disclosure and ambivalence on the boss' subjective judgment. The worry is that sensitive issues like appraisals, increments and promotions could be affected in the future. There is some distrust also with anonymous polls and hotlines, a worry that they may not remain quite as anonymous as they promise.

Fortunately, there are now considerable resources available outside the organizational set up for individuals to access. There are counsellors, career and life coaches and online platforms for further learning. Smitha Shetty is a career designer coach at Self-ActualizeLife.com, co-founder of an initiative called Parivartan-Empower Against Abuse and is currently based in Boston. She has taken several career breaks and recalls the generosity of her batchmates and even strangers she reached out to for advice and help. 'After each break, I came back to a better role and a higher salary,' she says. Smitha had the courage to ask for help and she was able to get it.

'Earlier professionals had less control and say over their careers and were dependent on their companies for their professional development,' says Minaxi Indra, business leader and president, UpGrad for Business. 'The EdTech (educational technology) sector has seen exponential growth partially in response to this need. Through an online learning platform, one can have access to some of the best universities and professors from around the world, including, multilingual content, blended learning with online and self-paced learning experiences, and a personalized learning experience without geographical barriers and at a fraction of the cost. Now, people can upgrade their skills or learn new ones without taking too much time away from their jobs and at little cost, with or without official sanction. Companies themselves are seeing the value in EdTech for up-skilling their talent, increasing employee engagement, retaining employees and saving on their training budgets,' she adds.

R.R. Nair believes transition points, particularly, need to be handled sensitively. He says, 'When people start their career, when they move from being individual contributors to team leaders and when they move into senior management, the pipeline of responsibility shifts and the skills, mindsets and behaviours required to manage it effectively also shift. Disruptions in the business environment happen outside of the control of the individual. As you move to senior levels, you need to strategically and proactively prepare for a shift to a global mindset. It is vital for people to be prepared for the responsibilities, skills and behaviours that can lead to team growth.'

Making it to the senior level feels like an accomplishment, and it is, given the challenges that had to be faced in the previous stages. There is also a sense of relief and entitlement. The struggles are in the past; the rewards are in the present. Free from the flexibility stigma, senior management professionals can not only take advantage of all the available benefits but also make new demands for customized ones. There are few who would care to question or stop them. They can now try to correct the imbalances in their personal lives.

Leadership has its perks, but it also has its pressures—responsibility for results and performance at a macro level, performing to the demands of the role, critical decision making and projecting the right image are some of them. It is also a lonely position, where it's difficult to tell how much of the admiration and appreciation belongs to the person and how much is due to the position. Despite their winning stance in the game, there is still some insecurity and threat perception. If it is not handled well, it can come out in ego-directed behaviours that are encouraged by tolerance due to high status in the hierarchy. It's like the story of the emperor's new clothes—how will he know he's naked if no one dares to tell him?

Sociopaths and predators are not exclusive to the corporate world, but to some extent, our cultural vulnerabilities leave a door open for extreme situations like corruption, fraud and sexual harassment. When a boss is the instigator, not only are we reluctant to call it out but we may also not allow ourselves to see it and/or believe it. Things difficult to say in person are even more challenging and liable to miscommunication and misinterpretation when relayed using technology, especially in remote-working situations.

The COVID-19 pandemic has been especially challenging for leaders. It was a disruption that came out of nowhere and threatened their businesses and employees like nothing else ever had. It didn't matter whether the leadership was employee-centric or not, digitally ready or not, agile and flexible or not—every organization had to react, learn and adapt fast to deal with the unprecedented situation. Many leaders admit that their response in some cases has been contextual, that they had no option but to cut costs and jobs, and that even as they gathered resources to support their employees, they could not shift their focus or reduce the pressure to achieve business outcomes. While the leaders still wonder how long the COVID situation will last and whether the changes it brought about will endure, they hope to at least carry forward the empathy they have developed.

Towards the end of a journey, we tend to look back, and we find our narrative coloured by the low and high points that stick in our memories. To someone at the beginning or at the losing end of the game, the obstacles in their way can still seem insurmountable. To those at the winning end, the same obstacles are reframed as necessary growth opportunities that helped them get there. It is the winning end that gets to call the shots for the rest of the game. So, why would we change anything that worked for us? We have less sympathy for people who are still stuck or stumbling; we feel they need to toughen up and learn the lessons we did. We don't see the need to make the game any easier for them than it was for us.

Ashok Capoor says, 'Even though the hierarchical culture still exists in the corporate world, the freshers today are far more questioning of the ways of doing business and are less afraid of the consequences. Their approach is to move on if they do not find a congenial working place. The seniors are still stuck in the old ways and find it difficult to manage these more questioning ways as well as the high attrition levels. HR departments are working overtime to find balanced solutions to manage the new expectations of the freshers and get them to converge with those of the seniors.'

At the senior level, future career decisions are subject to personal and family priorities. Dropping out of the corporate game at this point is not so common, but it may happen for personal rather than professional reasons. Retirement planning is more concrete with the recognition that neither health nor productivity is expected to decline significantly. While some look forward to more free time and travelling, most want to find ways to remain busy and feel valued.

The stage of retirement is difficult initially, with some loss of status and the trappings that go with it. This transition is cushioned with financial security and the demand for the kind of expertise that can only come from vast experience. The difficulty of managing administrative tasks and keeping up with technology has some solutions and the fear of obsolescence is addressed through a renewed spirit of learning and networking. They reach out to give and are also able to acknowledge what they receive. There is a freedom and flexibility that is ultimately enjoyed, along with a return to authenticity and a new sort of humility because all the value and appreciation they derive at this stage is entirely due to themselves and not to some position in the corporate hierarchy. At last, there is a comfortable point where the fear of the snakes does not fuel insecurity and the lure of the ladders does not drive impatience as this is not a point in the game at all. This is what comes after the game has run its course and now there is no destination left to seek, only a continuing journey to be savoured in the comfort already achieved.

Our status obsession has us placing our bosses on pedestals and being comfortable when our subordinates do the same to us, and this reinforces the high power distance[1] in our culture,

---

[1] Power distance is a dimension in the Hofstede Model of Cultural Dimensions, an anthropological tool used for cultural analysis. It is defined by Hofstede as the degree of inequality that exists – and is accepted – between people with and without power. India scores a high 77 on the Power Distance Index (PDI) versus the global average score of 59, indicating an appreciation for hierarchy and top-down structures in society and organizations.

Sources: https://clearlycultural.com/geert-hofstede-cultural-dimensions/power-distance-index/

https://www.hofstede-insights.com/country/india/

separating and isolating the cohorts in a way that disables the free flow of information, ideas and feedback. This is further hampered by the pandemic situation, which has increased the physical distance and communication challenges.

Our personal and professional lives cannot be easily separated now, and the flexibility stigma is still perceived to extract a price for every concession we take. Competition and distrust make for a prickly work environment where we are so often afraid to share our vulnerabilities or ask for help. So, our insecurities flourish. Seniors against juniors, women against men, peers against each other—every conceivable division is ammunition for our biases and suspicions. It's a struggle to swim against the tide, but we see the rewards as rich for those few who do. For so many of us, it's just about managing to keep our heads above the water till we reach the shore, where we take a quick breath before plunging back in, driven as we are to compete. There seems to be some residual fatalism in our belief that we only need to become better at playing the game rather than questioning some of its rigid rules.

Many years ago, a joke was popular among corporate circles comprising Indians and non-resident Indians. It's about a marine products exporter who gets a call from one of his overseas clients. The client is unhappy with his latest shipment of crabs. One of the containers, he says, was left open. He is livid at the irresponsibility as he would have lost a lot of money and time had the crabs escaped. The exporter is unfazed by this incident. He points out that the crabs would not have escaped because they are Indian crabs—if one were to climb up to the top of the container, it would be pulled back down by the others before it could escape.

If we look beyond the humour, this joke points to an unfortunate flaw in our cultural mindset. Some of us are conditioned from an early age to be extremely competitive, to want advantages for ourselves and disadvantages for our peers, to define success only within a relative context. The hard work we demand of ourselves is progressively increased by the efforts of our peers and the pressure to perform better than them. This drives us to chase perfection, which rationally we may know will never quite be in our grasp, but emotionally, we allow it to make us feel like we're never good enough.

'Thanks to our evolutionary brains, we are wired to look for negatives,' says Kalyani Capoor. 'This neurological bias is further reinforced by a culture that is fiercely competitive. The scarcity mentality is ingrained from a very young age and understandably so. Schools, colleges, jobs, promotions, all seem like a very finite pie and if someone gets a large slice of it there is that much less left for others. Is competition an unavoidable, even essential element of any social structure? Yes. And does competition stimulate the brain to be more alert, motivated and therefore, productive? Yes. These neurological benefits however are not only wiped out totally but also replaced by tremendous neurological cost when this competition is neither age appropriate nor healthy. The biggest cost of unhealthy competition is that it renders the environment psychologically unsafe and the human brain needs safety to be its best version over any sustained period of time.'

We can only have a high status if there are many others with a lower one. It prevents us, when we are higher up in the hierarchy, from changing the things that bothered us when we were lower down. The view is different from the top, and we want to enjoy it. It may not be the adverse situations that helped us, but the choices we made in how to handle them. 'We made it' is the justification for perpetuating the wrongs of our culture, that is, if we think about it at all. Quite often, we are just too busy to reflect and introspect.

What if our cultural strengths could be harnessed to make our corporate careers and lives better? We need the structure of a hierarchy, but do we need it to be so rigid that we lose meaningful information and fresh ideas to self-consciousness and censorship? If only we could bring the flexibility, ingenuity and spirit of compromise and cooperation that benefit us in our personal lives, despite our obvious biases, into our professional ones. If only we could see our colleagues more as collaborators rather than only as ruthless competitors. If we could allow that everyone, not just ourselves, should be able to access the things that make life worthwhile—meaningful work, just rewards and a sense of balance in our health, relationships and other interests that contribute to our overall well-being. This is something we need at every stage to be able to play the game, learn from our mistakes and pace ourselves for a real win.

PART 4
EXPERT REFLECTIONS

16

Reframing Success

Kalyani Capoor, Psychotherapist

The pursuit of success in urban India, by and large, begins early in life. Very often, it's a race that we run even before we really learn to walk.

Our definition of success, more often than not, is borrowed and introjected during our formative years.

The scarcity mindset is a worldview that resources and opportunities are very limited and in a third-world culture, it is more than a mere mindset. The competition, then, to be the best and grab the largest slice of a very finite pie is hardwired into us. As we grow older, our achievements start to become our identities, and our scores our self-worth. We learn these equations early and we learn them well since they are reinforced every step of the way.

Our definition of success, then, is understandably relative. We constantly compare ourselves to our peers and strive to be better than them in acquiring what our immediate and extended cultures endorse as concrete and legitimate measures of success—status and wealth.

Given this one-dimensional definition, success, like Zelus, becomes a ruthless god demanding an obsessive worship that disallows homage to any other altar but one. Our health, both physical and emotional, takes a back seat; our relationships become distant, superficial and transactional, and our sense of meaning and purpose at work and in life struggle to even find a place on our priority list.

The Associated Chambers of Commerce and Industry of India (ASSOCHAM), a non-governmental trade association and advocacy group, did a study in 2015 involving 1,250 employees from 150 companies.[1] It reported that 42.5 per cent of the employees showed signs of general anxiety disorder or depression. The incidence of anxiety and depression among corporate employees increased 45–50 per cent during 2008–15, and nearly 38.5 per cent of those surveyed slept less than six hours—which is a major contributing factor to depression and hypertension. YourDost, a technology-based counselling service, cites another 2015 report that states 50 per cent of corporate India is under chronic stress, with 30 per cent having problems such as addiction and marital discord and 20 per cent suffering from depression.[2] These statistics predate the COVID-19 pandemic, which we know has only compounded this issue.

That this data from ASSOCHAM is worrisome goes without saying. What it throws up is an almost inexplicable dissonance when we pair it with data gleaned from neuroscience. Neuroscience affirms that the human brain, a complex network of 80 billion neurons, is the most evolved of brains and has the largest cerebral cortex, which is capable of amazing feats

[1] Nandana James, 'Mental health: The elephant in the rooms of corporate India', *The Hindu Businessline*, December 2019, https://www.thehindubusinessline.com/blink/cover/mental-health-the-elephant-in-the-rooms-of-corporate-india/article30211327.ece

[2] YourDost, https://yourdost.com/blog/2016/04/causes-of-stress-in-india.html?q=/blog/2016/04/causes-of-stress-in-india.html&

of analysis, problem-solving and innovation. Studies in neuroplasticity have borne out the human brain's ability to grow and change in response to appropriate stimulation at any age. The dissonance that these two data points throw up is intriguing. Man has tamed technology, invented artificial intelligence and invaded outer space, but it is the inner space that continues to be a challenge.

So, is the human brain not as magnificent a machine as it is touted to be and/or aren't status and wealth valid measures of success and worth pursuing? The answers to both these questions are interlinked.

It's not the machine that seems at fault then, it's the mechanic. Most of us know much more about our mobile phones than our minds, and this neural machine does not come with a manual.

There are four fascinating but little-known facts about the human brain.

a. The first is that the brain is flexible or 'plastic' and has the ability to change and grow in response to new learning and stimulation (both internal and external) throughout life. Contrary to popular belief, the human brain is capable of making new neural connections at any age.
b. Secondly, the brain is a chemical factory, and our neurochemicals determine our physical health, energy, motivational levels and emotional well-being. Coming as it does from a large family of over forty neurotransmitters, cortisol deserves the credit for being the most commonly known. Also known as the stress hormone, cortisol is released in response to threat perception. More about this misunderstood molecule later.

   The good news is that we also have the quartet of chemicals that act as de-stressors and make merry melodies.

These are: 1) Dopamine (the motivation molecule), a pleasure chemical that plays a motivational role in the brain's reward system and helps with goal-oriented behaviour and decision-making; 2) Oxytocin (the bonding molecule), which is responsible for genuine bonding and reciprocal relationships; 3) Serotonin (the self-esteem molecule), which is a mood stabilizer that regulates sleep and digestion and boosts social confidence; 4) Endorphin (the 'feel good' molecule) that acts as a powerful painkiller and creates an euphoric feeling.

What is truly interesting and empowering is the fact of reciprocal influence: while the neurochemicals influence our cognitive and emotional well-being, our thoughts and activities in turn influence the level of these brain chemicals in our system. In other words, by altering our thoughts and activities, we can actually alter our brain chemistry for better or worse.

c. The third fact is that the brain finds it difficult to differentiate clearly between objective reality and subjective thinking about that reality. The mere thought of eating your favourite food is enough to trick the brain to produce saliva in much the same way that the actual smell and taste of that food would. This explains the 'placebo' effect and the effectiveness of sham surgeries. Thoughts and images click chemical switches in the brain, which in turn determine our physical and emotional well-being. Hence, what we think, imagine and visualize is of critical significance. The most powerful 'conversations' are the ones we have with ourselves.

d. And the final fact is that the human brain is evolutionary and is, therefore, wired to look for negatives. While we have the most evolved cortices across species, we still do have the residual reptilian brain, which played a critical role in the survival of our animal ancestors. This reptilian brain, called the amygdala, is the core of a neural system for processing fearful and threatening stimuli. Its job is to detect threat and activate reactions (fight, flee or freeze) to deal with that threat. Our animal ancestors were constantly surrounded by life-or-death dangers such as carnivores and forest fires. Amygdalic activation and hyper-vigilance were required in order to survive. It is, then, this animal brain that gets activated even today every time a threat is perceived by us.

The chemical warrior, cortisol, wakes up to this clarion call. Blood pressure, blood sugar and heart rate are elevated; blood starts to coagulate (lest there is a blood bath); the immune system is suppressed, and hyper vigilance sets in as the oxygen to the cortex is reduced. The amygdala hijacks our brain since survival seems to be at stake.

Cortisol is our ally in matters of life or death. For our animal ancestors, being eaten up by a carnivore or getting burnt by a forest fire were very real possibilities. The stakes for them were literally life or death, and the amygdalic activation was a survival mechanism.

Once the threat is dealt with, cortisol levels go back to normal.

What happens if this emergency response refuses to shut down and the warrior doesn't ever get to sheath his sword? That is when our survival mechanism goes horribly wrong. That is when our ally morphs into a monster. Prolonged elevated cortisol levels compromise our immunity, rob us of our sleep and take a toll on our cardiac health. Stress becomes our constant companion, sabotaging our concentration and confidence. More often than not, we turn to food, alcohol and substances to 'cope' with this, which further adds to the chaos, which is slowly becoming the order of the day. The stage is set for panic, anxiety and depression. The survival mechanism now endangers the very survival it was designed to protect.

The forest fires and the man-eating tigers are not our everyday threats anymore, and we have in our camp an incredibly evolved and competent cortex and yet, the stress statistics among Indians in general and Indian corporates in particular seem to indicate a collective amygdalic activation.

So, what is it other than life or death that is perceived as life or death? Every time an amygdala perceives a threat, it has no option but to swing into action and hijack the brain by holding the cortex hostage. And when the cortex is put on the back burner, the brain's ability to process data, to deduce and induce and to initiate appropriate action is significantly compromised. The hyper vigilance of the amygdala comes at a great cost, and while the elevated cortisol levels may well prepare us to fight, flee or freeze, they do precious little to help us survive, let alone thrive on a consistent basis in the corporate congos.

What are our forest fires today? Every time we perceive a threat to our self-worth, the emergency response is mobilized. Given our evolutionary brains, we are anyway wired to look for negatives. A brain that is wired for negatives and a work environment that's driven by pressure and unrealistic standards of self-worth pave the way to constant stress and worse. What defines our self-worth then is of central significance.

Our definition of self-worth, more often than not, comes from our early experiences and cultural conditioning. In a typical Indian education system, academic scores become our self-worth and our ranks among peers define our identities. And those measures of educational achievements translate seamlessly to wealth and status in a corporate context. My pay and perks are now my self-worth and my status my identity. And we come to the question that is very often raised in my group work with corporates: are wealth and status invalid measures of success? Is pursuit of success the problem?

Realizing our potential and acquiring and utilizing our skill sets to achieve success is, in fact, at the heart of personal fulfilment and social progress. That success and wealth are valid goals to work for is a given, and that they don't necessarily translate into happiness is also an indisputable fact. The pursuit of success is not the problem. The problem is with our definition of success.

Conventional measures of success are, unfortunately, limited to position, power and money; and our net worth is expressed in nothing but numbers. Integral intangibles such as healthy relationships with the self and others, physical and emotional well-being, the meaning we find in our work and our lives and our ability to savour and celebrate the present have no place in this myopic definition.

So, while designations and materialistic assets are valid measures of success, our current collective definition of success focuses exclusively on these and is, therefore, skewed and limited. It is only when our definition of success expands to include the intangible integrals that we find that the formula 'success = happiness' stands valid and vindicated.

The focus then shifts from being a successful banker or lawyer or CEO to being a successful human being, who duly honours every deity at life's altar.

At the core of this revised definition of success is the concept of balance. The workaholic who's strapped to a treadmill with no stop button is as much in a state of imbalance as the drifter who refuses to venture out of his comfort zone and participate. While the first extreme is often glorified and the second frowned upon, both extremes are far removed from that sane place of balance.

It is this balance that needs to be factored into our balance sheets when we evaluate our net worth.

While this revised definition of success sounds humane, holistic and even politically correct, it would, as it should, raise many a corporate eyebrow. If a system (leaders) bought, endorsed and reinforced this definition, wouldn't the productivity and profits plummet? This is a valid question and deserves an honest answer. And the answer seems to come from the sterile corridors of neuroscience rather than some nebulous new-age philosophy.

This definition of success centres on balance, and if adopted, it would inevitably translate into a corporate culture that not only believes in work-life balance for its employees but also insists on it. Research[3] shows that work-life balance, which factors in the intangible integrals, helps us become the best neural versions of ourselves.

When a leader redefines success, both his and others', to include health, relationships, meaning and purpose at work and in life, he creates an environment of trust and contributes to the collective well-being of the team. He invests in his own inner emotional health, which in turn allows him to steer clear of favouritism, domination and destructive criticism. He is aware enough to know his flaws and courageous enough to own them. He's strong enough to be in touch with his own vulnerability and secure enough to give credit where it is due. Work becomes a place of trust for the employees and a place where they feel acknowledged, guided and valued.

A leader can literally alter the collective brain chemistry of his team, and he can do this by enlisting the help of the chemical quartet mentioned earlier.

---

[3] Kristine Gill, 'This is What Checking Email After Work Does to Your Brain', *Real Simple*, 29 December 2021. Available at https://www.realsimple.com/work-life/life-strategies/job-career/after-hours-emails-impact-mental-health.

In trustworthy environments, people feel safe and interact authentically. This gets oxytocin flowing. When their efforts and inputs are recognized and openly appreciated, serotonin is stimulated. In the face of challenging but realistic goals, their brains release dopamine and when work-life balance frees up their time and energy for fitness routines and meaningful hobbies, endorphins are released.

The combined force of the chemical quartet benefits their health, raises their energy levels, sharpens their memory and concentration, boosts their confidence and enhances their motivation and decisiveness.

The quartet of neurotransmitters act as powerful de-stressors and contribute to a person's overall well-being.

On a healthy diet of this chemical soup, the human brain becomes its best version: energetic, sharp, ethical and motivated. The collective attitude and behaviour of the team is primarily driven by rational cortical centres rather than anxious amygdalas. Productivity and profits, far from shrinking, may burst at the seams.

One may ask if it is the leader who has the power to define and determine the culture within an organization; doesn't that absolve the individual employee of all ownership? After all, marching to the beat of one's own drum may not be just difficult but can even end up being disastrous. The fact that the leader/system has the power to shape culture does not free us of our personal responsibility.

We are at our effective best when we are able to distinguish between what is under our direct control and what is not and invest our energies accordingly. This helps us move from our area of concern to our area of influence. We focus on building our immunity rather than the toxins in our environment. We begin to invest in our physical and mental health and in our relationships with others, and most importantly, in our relationship with ourselves. We become aware of our borrowed definitions of self-worth and success and our own amygdalic triggers.

Poor self-esteem and perfectionistic standards prompt us to make inaccurate appraisals of everyday demands at work. We perceive threats where there are none or, at best, magnify them out of proportion. Our catastrophic self-talk and imagined worst-case scenarios further fuel the fire since the brain takes them seriously. We feel overwhelmed, anxious and powerless. We are then likely to react from the amygdala (fight, flee, freeze) rather than respond from our higher cortical centres that are solution-oriented and highly rational. These reactions are, more often than not, exaggerated and inappropriate. The others around us respond to our reactive behaviour negatively, which further undermines our fragile sense of self-worth, thus setting a vicious cycle in motion.

Challenging our self-sabotaging beliefs and self-talk and substituting these with rational ones goes a long way in keeping our brain chemistry healthy and helpful. When we take charge of what is under our control, 'what is not' begins to shift and change. This is reciprocal power.

Research seems undivided in indicating that when we invest in our physical and mental health, when we value and nurture genuine relationships, when we allow ourselves to take healthy pride in and celebrate our small wins and permit ourselves to truly exhale from time to time, our productivity peaks rather than plummets.

Honouring every deity at life's altar seems to enhance our worship of work rather than take away from it, and life then becomes a meaningful experience to be savoured and celebrated rather than an anxious performance waiting endlessly for applause!

17

Leadership Behaviour and Influence

Ashok Capoor, Business Consultant

There are many theories of leadership. Leadership coaches, training and books are abundant, but it is up to each individual leader to develop his/her own leadership style. There are many factors that could affect leaders—their individual personalities, values and life experiences to the kind of leadership they have been exposed to in their careers.

Being a leader is not an easy task as leaders are under tremendous pressure today. They are legally liable for every small and big action of the company. They have to answer to directors and investors on business performance, to the market on sustainability and diversity and to the employees on work culture and rewards. Their reputations are vulnerable to social media and official as well as unofficial feedback systems.

Self-management to team management is a difficult as well as an on-going transition. Managing their own stress needs to be a priority for leaders or else they will end up passing it down to their colleagues. How leaders manage and handle stress also send signals to the other employees about how they may address their own. Leaders need to ensure they have time for self-care and reflection so that they can develop a sharper self-awareness, which is essential to be an effective and good leader.

Early in my leadership career, I had a deputy who was a bit blunt. Once, one of his juniors had asked for leave as his wife was very ill. The deputy refused to give his permission, saying that as the junior was not a doctor, his role in his wife's illness was limited. Unfortunately, the junior's wife died; then the entire staff was up in arms against the deputy and wanted his resignation for his insensitive behaviour. On my insistence, he gave a written apology to the entire team and promised to be more compassionate in the future.

The lesson is very clear that just because you are in a position of power, you cannot ride roughshod and be insensitive to your juniors' needs. These are lessons learnt the hard way, but the sad part is that very few senior managers realize the importance of compassion and often use their power without any qualms to get their juniors to do their bidding. With the backdrop of the pandemic, it is all the more important to be careful how you deal with your juniors. Many organizations provide anonymous feedback on their bosses so that senior management can guide managers to ensure proper behaviour in the organization.

The status hierarchy being culturally important, bosses will always get due respect, even if it is on the surface level. Genuine respect needs to be earned through action and impact. Leaders who rely on their status alone may find that their juniors, while outwardly polite and deferential, do not put in much effort for them or for the organization.

It is a tightrope walk trying to extract performance from your juniors without really getting on their case. However, if your juniors believe in you in the real sense of the term, then they will require minimum monitoring and most of them will ensure best performance themselves. Once they start to believe that it is their own company, the motivation starts coming from within. To achieve this, it is of the utmost importance that you get in the shoes of your juniors, understand their issues and mentor them accordingly based on their strengths and weaknesses. Every employee does not respond the same way, some need more monitoring and guidance, and some need more autonomy. It is critical to build trust and have room for making and learning from mistakes.

Leaders need to develop clarity for themselves on what they want the organizational culture to be. Transparent, authentic, rational and objective feedback systems can create a nurturing environment that encourages learning and promotes a real understanding of what the company values and seeks to promote in its internal culture. Diversity in hiring brings up different points of view, thereby enriching the overall decision-making, leading to better outcomes. Leaders need to create an environment where all the employees feel they have a voice and that their voices will be, and are, heard. More rational and fearless feedback leads to decisions based on reality and objectivity rather than the poor-quality decisions that result from inauthentic feedback when employees feel they must say or not say certain things to please their bosses.

The important thing is to have not just the right policies but also the right perceptions and actions that convey that the company really cares and is doing the right thing. When people feel that the right people are being promoted or given better increments, it builds a sense of fairness and equity, which is important to counterbalance the inherent ambition and competition, helping develop feelings of belonging and ownership in employees.

The COVID-19 pandemic has enforced a faster-than-comfortable adoption of digitization and remote working. Like every work-organization option, these have their pros and cons, and we are learning about them through trial and error. Work from home has become a reality, which many conservative companies find very difficult to manage. This is mainly because they believe that people do not work as seriously from home as they would from an office. This is a wrong perception as many people are actually working more hours from home, putting in some of the time and energy saved from their daily work commutes. There is also evidence of more fatigue from a blurring of any physical boundaries between work and personal life, with even less time and space to adjust between the two. Trust between leaders and their employees is all the more critical in this scenario, and it is my personal view that some face-to-face interaction is essential to build that trust. Leaders need to keep a balance in the work environment so that the personal touch and bonding among employees are not completely lost to digitization.

The pressure on CEOs to deliver results every quarter is palpable, and this corresponds to the pressure exerted on them by their boards. Leaders at all levels are under tremendous duress to show short-term results, and they find the easiest way to do this by cutting costs. Therefore, there is a relentless pressure to cut costs in terms of overheads, personnel, travel etc. Cutting costs in such a manner is quite unhealthy since, apart from cutting flab in the system, most leaders end up cutting necessary support, like budgets for training, mentoring and team-bonding activities. This may hurt the business in the long run as productivity suffers due to lack of adequate manpower, business relationships becoming transactional etc. It requires exceptional strength for leaders to take a balanced view and keep the company's long-term sustainability in mind while taking steps to shore up short-term profits. In the pandemic, while most companies cut costs drastically by removing manpower etc., the Tatas and some other companies did not sack people but gave regular increments. This led to improvement in productivity and improved the results of the business when the business cycle turned the corner.

New processes that have emerged due to digitization have changed the way work is done and, in turn, have created more redundancies. The loss of jobs is a serious issue and has led to a lot of insecurity among people. Insecurity leads to tremendous stress, which lowers productivity. Leaders need to ensure that most of the existing employees are retained, and layoffs are minimized. Also, if they behave in a more humane manner, they will have greater loyalty and productivity that will more than compensate for the extra short-term costs. In fact, as I mentioned earlier, it is in times of crisis that a company's leadership can have a positive impact. During the COVID-19 pandemic crisis, Infosys did not sack any employee and ensured good increments to their salaries. This has led to a greater level of loyalty and positive word-of-mouth for the company. People have realized that it is preferable to work for a company that cares for them, and this will probably lower Infosys's attrition levels in the near future.

Compassionate leaders who demonstrate empathy along with leadership get more loyalty and better performance from their employees than autocratic leaders. And they recognize that a healthy and happy workforce is more productive. Corporates that encourage a skew towards workaholism and reward only work are not healthy in the real sense. Throughout my career, I consistently left the office at 5.30 p.m. My bosses were not too happy but could not stop me because I completed my work each day and delivered good results. I always told my juniors that if they worked long hours, it meant that they were not being productive. Hard work by itself means nothing; working smart is good for the company and for the individual. Encouraging employees to balance time for themselves and their families is in the company's best interests. Unhappy employees can seriously disrupt or infect the work environment and have a negative cascading effect on the work culture. Employees who have good personal relationships also have better professional connections and relationships that lead to a healthier work environment. Such people can also be a good resource for the company's business development.

Leadership roles force multiple perspectives on individual leaders. They are employees themselves, with their own personal responsibilities to manage and balance alongside their weighty work responsibilities. They also need to develop and manage healthy, productive teams and have the opportunity to drive the organizational culture in the direction they choose. They are role models for other employees who look up to them for their own aspirations and try to imbibe the desired values and behaviours that could lead them to that position. In fact, managers might implicitly and instinctively discount ideas that feature in their organizations' internal policies. So, leaders have to work hard on themselves in pursuit of the company's interests, not just by motivating other employees and creating the culture they seek but also by living and breathing it.

18

The Organizational View and Role of HR

R.R. Nair, HR Consultant

From the many true stories chronicled in this book, it is evident that there are many themes of disruptions of joy and happiness that were already present at work in Indian corporate offices in pre-pandemic times. I believe some of them are self-imposed, which, for a few people, are motivated by extrinsic factors like money versus intrinsic satisfaction at work for others in terms of their sense of purpose and value. The unwillingness to become more self-aware and take control of situations through self-mastery is one problem. Obsession with perfection is another common theme, with self-imposed standards of excellence that may tend towards performance anxiety. Another cause of disruption is interpersonal conflicts, which lead to self-doubt and an increasing level of toxicity. The stress related to an inability to handle multi-tasking and effectively manage time and the inability to handle pressure is also very common.

Besides these self-imposed challenges, which are often not on the conscious plane, disruptions of happiness also occur when bosses tend to be control freaks, unmindful of their lack of empathy and self-control. This sort of task centricity often combined with lack of a clear vision and purpose, arising out of a short-term view, tends to alienate people from purposeful engagement. In fact, all these factors hasten disengagement. Employees' discretionary efforts and contributions come down drastically. This is a bit of a vicious cycle. People's engagement and productivity come down. Bosses become even more tense and feel pressured to achieve stretch goals and targets. The more they fail, the more they control and micromanage their people resulting in lower morale and team commitment. The over-scheduled calendars for leaders leave less time for engagement with employees in an informal manner. People eventually feel that they don't matter or factor into the organizational priorities. Eventually, this leads to undesirable levels of exits. We keep hearing about good employees who may not be planning to leave good companies but will quit when they encounter a bad boss.

Why is it important for a boss to understand employee motivations? What shapes and influences the changing needs at various life stages in one's career? How do leaders create a vision? Do they believe in co-creating it or driving it down the throat? Shared vision is purposeful and motivating. People follow the vision co-created by leaders whom they trust. And vision and action when combined can transform the organization and its culture. Increasingly, disengagement happens, especially with high-quality young talent, when they find that the leadership is only paying lip service towards a larger cause that the organization and its people have collectively identified with. There are many good causes connected with the society in which we live and function. However, much of the time, the needs of the community are not well understood and fully aligned within the purpose of the organization.

In addition, the pandemic has impacted our daily life in unprecedented ways. People have reported significant changes in sleep patterns and challenges in prioritizing tasks, distinguishing between personal time and work time, leading to little or no physical activity, increase in anxiety levels, and impaired coping abilities. All these have contributed to higher stress levels and, consequently impacted employee well-being. Organizations that I know of have become acutely aware of their role in providing support to employee groups to cope with these changes. HR professionals have become more sensitive to this situation, and quite a few of them have been keen to understand more deeply the phenomenon of well-being and what needs to be done to create a culture shift in terms of showing more empathy towards employees both at the individual and at the group level. Many webinars on the relationship between changes in lifestyle habits and anxiety conditions pointed out that there is a strong correlation between the two. People are getting disoriented, safety and health-related concerns are becoming dominant, often rising to an obsessive-compulsive level, and evidence of withdrawal symptoms resulting from the increasing distance between co-workers is widespread. Consequently, there is a feeling of alienation and loss of self-control, as well as a lack of sense of direction, leading to the urgent need for restoring a locus of control in life and work.

Besides the impact of the pandemic on sales, cash flows, customer services and business operations, I have noticed that most organizations have lived up to their expectations by going out of the way to ensure the safety of employees and their families. These efforts included emergency medical support, arranging food and medical supplies for those affected, extending support to those grieving the loss of near and dear ones and to communities around factory establishments, organization of vaccination campaigns in collaboration with governmental and social organisations, and ensuring support for the health emergency staff to keep essential services going.

Organizing remote working involved providing provision for appropriate IT enabled tools and helping employees to adjust to new ways of working. Initially, there were concerns about a fall in productivity and how to buy into productivity-measuring software tools. Soon, many employers started trusting their employees as they discovered that performance efficiency did not drop as drastically as was expected.

The pandemic has taught people to stop immobilizing oneself, to find ways and means to liberate the self from self-limiting thoughts and behaviours and to explore and expand one's horizons. This is a shift from being obsessed with constraints and threats to seizing opportunities and identifying possibilities. People have started to see the difference between what cannot be accomplished and what can be accomplished. People have awoken from an immobilized sense of inertia, shifting from being pessimistic towards more optimistic attitudes, from a fixed mindset to a growth mindset. Reinvent and re-imagine have become the focus words in our new lexicon.

The pandemic has also taught us some fresh lessons for managing others. There is a realization that, just like the four wheels of a car, there are four wheels in our life: the physical, the mental, the emotional and the spiritual. As long as these four are balanced, one can expect a relatively smoother ride in both life and work. Amidst the COVID-19 crisis, our attitudes have now become more caring, more open to sharing and growing together than ever before. Health, well-being and safety concerns as well as the emergence of WFH are now better established.

One important positive consequence has been the realization of the importance of reaching out to skip-level employees. Initiating skip-level dialogues, especially with those who are new or dispersed or introverted, has resulted in creating a more psychologically safe environment for people to share their feelings. This is indeed a leveller, breaking away from the traditional hierarchical orientation of senior managers. The leader is a brand and like any brand, his or her availability and visibility are important. There is a greater realization that while accomplishing the task is important, it is equally important that there is an acceptance of the leader by the followers. This combination leads to effectiveness.

Several positive changes in corporate attitudes and behaviours have been reported; for example, greater levels of humility, empathy, respect and acceptance. As a result, reflective conversations are happening. People are inquiring about others to try and understand their personal and professional circumstances more appreciatively. Performance is one thing, but what drives people to perform has now become a special area of interest. Are people seeking money, task related structure, quality relationships at the workplace, recognition, the opportunity to exercise power and influence with a view to impact the outcome, or for pure intrinsic fulfilment? Yet, time and again we come across senior managers who have not spent adequate time and effort to understand more deeply what kind of needs people have.

Employees want to make a difference. There are many who express a desire to work for the community and social causes besides engaging with the primary task of the organization. Senior managers are beginning to detect the unsung heroes in their teams, and they say that there are many such shining examples at every level in the organization.

Teams' internal support structures help in deciding with speed over precision. There is less analysis paralysis. Business sustenance has become the key focus. Establishment of war rooms, empowerment of the front line and embracing action with commitment have augured well in creating a 'can do' spirit.

In my view, this is widespread in enlightened multinational corporations as well as founder-led Indian organizations.

Early in the pandemic, some organizations[1] even declared that WFH would be the future of work. Many felt that every job can be performed from home. Remote working and virtual working became buzzwords. This prevails among certain sections of employees, like individual contributors, especially in the software services industries even now. I am told that many employees, are questioning the need for offices. They advocate the virtues of saving the planet, lowering emissions, having better air quality with less traffic congestion as well as the positives of enormous savings on travel time, healthier lifestyles, greater family support, better quality attention to children and many other benefits. For many, WFH has become a revolutionary change.

Assessing the situation towards the end of 2021, what did I discern about the Bangalore scene? Almost 75 per cent of employees in IT/BT space were away from the city. They had dispersed to over a hundred cities and towns throughout the country. It appeared that they were not very inclined to return to their workplaces and forgo the considerable savings arising from not having to rent out a place, not having to commute as well as lower expenses on food and shopping.

Many HR leaders have examined the concept of WFH more deeply. They recognize that the pandemic has taught them that more work can be done remotely than they had originally visualized. This necessity has also compelled the creation of

[1] Anuj Tiwari, 'From Tata Steel To Microsoft, These Companies Have Shifted To Work From Home Permanently', *India Times*. Available at https://www.indiatimes.com/trending/social-relevance/companies-that-have-shifted-to-work-from-home-permanently-559054.html.

many productivity assessment tools during mid-2020, even though most organizations, as I said earlier, have gradually given them up due to the increased levels of responsibility from employees for delivering what is expected of them. As we cross over the third anniversary of the COVID-19 pandemic, it's a good time to take stock of our experiences with the quality and range of hardware, technology tools and smart-messaging tools we have provided to remote-working employees to facilitate working with them besides developing training for up-skilling and re-skilling employees; for example, training on virtual meeting skills.

Overall, we note that people are now comfortable enough to openly discuss the virtues of dispersed remote working, which has led to increased levels of individual productivity and commitment. HR and business leaders are also of the view that legacy metrics to assess performance need to be reviewed and new measures have to be developed and deployed for a virtual world that are better aligned with digital workflows. In fact, employees want to know how well they are doing even more often when they are stressed and challenged to perform better with less support. The key performance indicators need to be revisited to make sure that the dispersed and remote work actually delivers because a high-performance culture requires high-performance metrics as well. Along with these, the frequency of pulse surveys to assess employee engagement would also need to increase, and corrective actions following the findings would need senior leadership attention.

HR leaders are also examining the question of any downsides that need to be considered. For example, does continued WFH result in the reduction of team productivity especially while executing high-end work that requires intense collaboration between inter-disciplinary workforces? This is especially relevant for the functions of design, product engineering and product development. The power of teamwork cannot be underestimated. Teams facilitate the transfer of knowledge and, as we know, knowledge is power. Sharing knowledge enables others to act. The new business reality, post pandemic, will require greater-than-before team performance in order to grow and succeed in a fiercely competitive environment. We can leverage the power of teams better when we turn up physically at the workplace, get into a breakout room, challenge and support ideas from people with diverse orientations and backgrounds, and have informal conversations with colleagues and friends. The availability of specific infrastructure and state-of-the-art technology support systems on a 24/7 basis at the workplace also contribute towards generating innovations and out-of-the-box thinking.

Let's not forget what Aristotle said, 'Man is by nature a social animal.'[2] We value each other's company. The best innovative ideas come from adopting cross-functional perspectives in a stimulating work environment. Virtual working is not always a perfect substitute for Working from Office (WFO). The traditional office or workplace also provides a sense of pride for us. The physical setting serves as an archive with huge storage capacity in terms of myths and reality, stories about our successes and failures and what we learned from each one of them. Studies have shown that the workplace setting with its conference rooms, cafeteria, open spaces and lawns, individual workstations with personal artefacts and pin-ups of family portraits, recreation centres etc., enhances one's sense of identity and feeling of belonging to the organization. The facilities and their distinctiveness also attract people to the organization and help in retaining

---

[2] Sir Ernest Barker, *The Politics of Aristotle* (Oxford: Oxford University Press, 1995).

them, playing a critical role in our challenges relating to our current war for talent acquisition.

Senior HR leaders strongly advocate the importance of the workplace as a source of inspiration for learning and development. We learn a lot by watching others in the work setting, from team meetings, presentations and discussion forums and also by having informal sessions with our peers. In these days of constant disruptions in technology and market forces, we also learn from our juniors in casual settings outside the formal workspace like the wide-open campus spaces that many large organizations have.

One of the things that I used to love is the age-old practice of 'MBWA'—management by wandering around—which is especially useful for HR professionals and senior management to get a more accurate and acute sense of the company's work atmosphere and employee morale. How about a stroll around the park or the fountain, just before or after lunch? Or drop in on our teams for a chat or grab a coffee and walk into a room that has a whiteboard to ideate? We all know from experience that these inter-personal interactions not only build informal connections, but employees also learn from others' experience. These opportunities enable them to express their thoughts and improve their communication skills.

I like to use the letter T to illustrate that corporate employees need to develop both depth (the stem of the T) and breadth (the horizontal line) in their thinking. When we learn the corporate language, we also need to learn the nuances on how things get done in the corporate world, including both the formal and the informal dimensions of organization culture and mindset. We need to learn about the larger purpose of the organization, as stated in words as well as experienced in action. These cannot be absorbed merely from WFH. We will miss out on a lot in the long run if WFH becomes the norm.

A good question to ask ourselves now is whether we will be working remotely in the future or whether we will get back to the WFO of the pre-pandemic era? What is the likely scenario? A great deal of debate is going on regarding this and there is no-one-size-fits-all answer for every organization and every function. We know that there are varieties of tasks that are performed in an organization depending upon the nature of the industry and its customer profile. Manufacturing facilities are very clear about their stance: People have to be where there is a machine interface. Knowledge workers across professional service industries whose tasks need specialized expertise, especially at the individual contributor level, can and will probably move into a virtual mode. Periodically, they will have to gather at the workplace for all-hands meetings, or for an award and celebration event, or for a major client visit, or to be part of a fellowship to celebrate an annual event. In the case of team leaders who supervise individual contributors, and at the same time serve as the glue between heads of departments/functions/practice verticals and the individual contributors who are the front-end talent, they may represent what is now known as the 'hybrid workforce', a combination of WFH and WFO. Getting the team leaders to come together for a couple of days in a week would facilitate collaboration and a greater understanding of the context—the why of what we are doing. They can periodically share their ideas and experiences from their respective teams' WFH perspectives and consider how to strengthen its effectiveness. However, the heads of the departments and top leadership team members have already moved back into WFO mode last year.

One of the positive consequences of WFH is flexibility for employees. This has naturally directed a reservoir of talent to migrate to industries that offer this benefit. Qualified women may choose to enter the market in larger numbers for a career that offers flexible work time. This can accelerate gender diversity. HR processes need to become more flexible for hiring and deploying such talent. The HR function also has to find more creative ways to facilitate the onboarding of new recruits and provide them with virtual tours of the office and easier access to their managers. I have also encouraged senior HR leaders to adopt virtual mentoring, frequent leader-teach technology sessions, and fireside chat shows with senior leaders etc. Equally, organizations have commenced focusing on saving office space by creatively redesigning it. They are already conceiving fresh ideas around a 'phygital' infrastructure that may be the new reality for many of us.

There are, of course, downsides to WFH as well. There are many webinars and podcasts on this topic. The major one is stress due to violations of the boundaries that need to be maintained between the workspace and the home space. The increasingly blurred line between the two is disturbing. On top of it is the strain due to lack of social exposure, as pointed out earlier. We need to be more mindful of the nature of work and its many manifestations while planning ahead.

A pertinent question we could raise at this stage is whether we have gone too soft on people during the pandemic or whether we need to continue to strive for a balance between the organization's needs and the people's needs. Leaders are also facing an immense amount of pressure from investors and multiple stakeholders to perform and deliver results. This is the central paradox of the leadership challenge today. The answer cannot be either–or. I strongly believe it's always both. We all know that we need to understand people's needs and be prepared to act on them. Only then can we meet the organizational goals.

There are some related debates going on about whether the pandemic has overemphasized the importance of empathy and employee care in the role of managers and leaders at all levels.

We all know that poor leaders create disengaged employees. Effective leaders, on the other hand, create committed and engaged employees. These debates have engaged the attention of leadership experts, academic scholars and researchers.

In good times and in bad times, what helps in promoting employee engagement? There are effective leaders who advocate excellence in everything that people do, encourage the use of one's infinite potential to take stretch targets, communicate the business context effectively—more specifically the why of what we need to do—remove the blockers in terms of structural or resource-related impediments and encourage both continuous improvements and breakthroughs. There is also a section of effective managers and leaders who show tremendous empathy and who are rooted in humility. They are people who believe strongly in trusting and respecting others, showing a special ability to sense and respond to what is going on in the minds of their team members. They are sensitive to others' feelings, and are, above all, trustworthy. These kinds of leaders are capable of receiving feedback as well as in giving constructive and honest feedback to others, both to leverage their strengths and to address improvement areas. They constantly endeavour to develop their teammates and collaborate towards their success. In fact, they create a work culture to promote the psychological contracts that overlay and enhance the actual employment contracts between employees and the organizations, so that employees strive to put in discretionary efforts to contribute and to experience self-fulfilment. Many believe that in the post-pandemic scenario, both leadership styles in a combined form is likely to gain traction and will receive greater acceptance from employees and other stakeholders, especially in a globally competitive scenario. Not either–or, but both.

Recently we have been hearing about something called 'dashboard transparency'. Some employees are choosing to programme their laptops to provide a visual summary of how they have spent time at remote workstations or WFH, highlighting the time spent on sent and received messages, documents exchanged, meetings scheduled, planned and actual deliveries, feedback received, items from an open-item list closed during the day and priority tasks to be addressed the following day. They are sharing their screens with their colleagues with a view to be more transparent, to develop an interdependent spirit among team members and work more cohesively to create a sense of joy and vibrancy at the workplace. They believe that in this way they can create a culture to break away from silo thinking and hoarding of information, and work towards a common purpose that will enhance both productivity and job satisfaction. These innovations and best practices can fundamentally alter workflow and automation maps as well. Equally, digital tracking and monitoring platforms that provide laser-sharp analytic insights potentially help employees and leaders to take greater self-accountability for performance deliverables. Self-accountability in these times has assumed a great deal of importance. However, we must be mindful that these tools and platforms are used voluntarily and need an environment of trust among employees, a climate of inter-dependency and support to deliver to their potential. Many business leaders, HR practitioners and academia believe that the pandemic experience has undoubtedly hastened these indispensable developments. The intent with which they are deployed has to be clearly communicated to employees, and their decision to participate or not must not be coerced in any way. An inclusive and consensual approach is essential. If employees feel that there are respectful boundaries and safeguards for their privacy and autonomy, the increased collaboration could lead to a more joyful and energizing work environment. The 'smell of the place',[3] as aptly referred to by Sumantra Ghoshal, will then be invigorating.

Let me make a few final observations. Many of the most uncomfortable or rather painful experience-based life stories that have been chronicled in the book suggest that there is an acute need to humanize the organizations around the principles of fairness, equity and natural justice. Employees need managers and senior leaders who are fair, reasonable and ethical in their approach to tasks and people. And it's not enough for leaders to believe that they are being fair and reasonable, they also need to demonstrate this in action so that they are also seen to be fair within the organisation. Perception matters. The HR and line management together are custodians of a healthy culture. And in the rapidly changing world, employees need leaders who can treat data and analytics as enablers for people to grow and realize their potential. This would mean that managers and leaders should commit themselves to promote a feedback culture. Feedback on how well employees' need for new capability development and new learning are getting addressed, feedback on their professional and career growth and unconditional support to cope with their challenges at the workplace. HR needs to define and develop a shared perspective that is equally enabling and supportive for those who are working remotely, those who are skewed to WFO and those following a hybrid model. Credibility on performance management processes depends on transparency and openness. Employees must be able to identify the line of sight between their performance and contribution and the organization's awards, recognitions and celebrations, devoid of gender or other biases.

---

3 Sumantra Ghoshal, speech at the World Economic Forum, Davos 1995.

It is vital for leaders to better understand and identify their own unconscious biases. Therefore, it is necessary for structured interventions to provide opportunities for deeper self awareness, so that they can ensure greater diversity and inclusiveness within the organization and become strong advocates for fairness and equity.

The role of business leadership cannot be underestimated if the organization has to continue in perpetuity. Leaders and their HR teams need to actively manage the organizational climate to enhance employees' energies and build resilience during crisis situations. In the absence of this, growing pessimism, burnout syndromes and a lack of will to overcome obstacles will become palpable. HR has now assumed centre-stage in most organizations by championing more human-centric approaches that put people at the heart of institutional growth. The pandemic has, in fact, accelerated this new phenomenon. An increasing number of organizations are attempting to adopt a more humanistic approach while designing new ways of doing things, redesigning structures and processes, and engaging their people with a shared purpose.

Let me close this chapter by referencing a few additional roles of HR. For quite some time, the future of work and its impact on HR's role has been debated. The pandemic has accelerated the discussion. First, as was stated earlier, HR managed in unprecedented ways to keep the employees safe and supported many steps to ensure organizational survival. Remote work, business continuity plans, emergency communication processes, and preventive steps to safeguard both the mental and physical health of employees and often the families who needed attention, became the focal point. At present, HR is grappling with the challenges of developing the new normal. HR leaders are revisiting the competencies and mindsets required to succeed. And among the most frequently referred to are the adversity quotient, crisis management, learning agility and complexity management. The further challenge is how to identify, develop and cultivate the required mindset.

HR leaders have realized the need to collaborate closely with employees at all levels. This realization that they need to leverage the power of collective wisdom to cope with the complexities has brought in a culture of greater democratization of the workplace. Traditional thinking is giving way to more experimentation and creative disruptions in HR processes and policies. The culture of perceived bureaucracy is making way for more customized solutions, avoiding the trap of one-size-fits-all, and the practice of a leadership style is moving towards a coaching style, rooted in trust and empathy. From the employee's standpoint, a trusting relationship between the employee and the immediate manager is paramount to their job satisfaction. Research has established that a high-trust context encourages employees to become their true selves and promotes empowerment, which enable them to courageously seek creative ways to address their grievances and concerns. We all know that we are at our best when we feel happy and satisfied. There is a spring in our steps, and we have that vibrant, bouncy feeling that energizes and drives us to give our best. Everyone can learn to be more comfortable with their own vulnerabilities and become more authentic. Combined with this shift is the opportunity to leverage the core values of the organization. Organizations will then become institutions in perpetuity, and every individual will have a place in them.

19

Workspace Design

Rohit Krishan Gulati, Architect and Design Consultant

In 2017, Apple Inc. moved into its new headquarters — the Apple Park, in Cupertino, California. Steve Jobs had launched this project in 2011, a few months before his demise. It is a unique, ring-shaped building located on a site of 200 acres, with a built-up area of almost three million square feet to house over 12,000 employees.

Apple's decision to integrate several smaller offices and campuses into one big space is contrary to the way Silicon Valley companies have been evolving, i.e., having a network of corporate offices distributed among the commercial shops and public spaces of a neighbourhood community. Information technology (IT) workers in the Valley like to move freely through these different spatial contexts, bumping into colleagues, collaborators, potential partners and other urbanites. In the last decade, the speed and disruptive scale of the IT companies inevitably forced them to choose workspaces that emphasize extreme flexibility, impermanence, and the ability to be reconfigured to accommodate rapid growth. For the workers, the workplace is not a space built by 'furniture' but by a series of digital collaborative spaces connected by networks. Work happens anywhere and anytime within this urban fabric. It mirrors the nature of online interactions, where personal, social, and professional lives interconnect naturally at all hours.

The planning at Apple Park has been designed to develop a 'collaborative context'. This was done to promote increased proximity to one another and encourage face-to-face interactions, informal deal making and changeable, impermanent team and organizational structures. This has led to open floor plans, rich amenities and services, informal attire, a collegial atmosphere and the promotion of a very distinct work culture. The more successful interior spaces foster 'collisions' and spontaneous interactions among employees through a variety of space typologies. Those collisions, as several researchers have shown, should assist in increased learning, collaboration and ultimately innovation. It should also be stated that many researchers have advocated the contrary as well.

Steve Jobs's aspiration was 'a signature campus that expresses the values of the company for generations'.[1] In its passion to achieve it, Apple seems to have taken a retrograde step in emphasizing metrics, such as efficiency, cost, profitability per square foot and maintenance overheads, etc., which are generally taken into consideration by real estate developers. While not undermining the several unique architectural innovations and the benchmarks in energy efficiency and technical prowess achieved in Apple Park, the campus has been said to be hated due to its 'rigid layout' and 'snobbish character' and also as it forces employees to travel further than ever before. Internal

---

[1] Jennifer Magnolfi, 'Why Apple's New HQ Is Nothing Like the Rest of Silicon Valley', *Harvard Business Review*, June 2017. Available at https://hbr.org/2017/06/why-apples-new-hq-is-nothing-like-the-rest-of-silicon-valley.

layouts are said to be inflexible, and most employees are forced to sit in unidentifiable open-plan linear workstations, instead of cubicles, giving no privacy or quietness or sense of community to the teams. Of course, the company's top management have private offices and it is important to note that there was no childcare centre. Several teams had professed resistance to shift to the new premises.

In 2010, Hindustan Unilever Limited shifted its Mumbai corporate office to a new campus in Andheri East, moving from the landmark Lever House at Backbay Reclamation, where it had been housed for over forty-six years. The shift had been planned almost five years earlier, with a vision to integrate business processes and leverage scale and synergies across the organization. The legacy office was old, out-dated and getting increasingly expensive to maintain. The new office, called the HUL Campus, is spread over twelve and a half acres and accommodates more than 1,600 employees. Lever House was leased out and, ultimately, sold off at a high profit.

Before the shift, most of the HUL employees were commuting from the suburbs or central Mumbai to south Mumbai, so this northward shift of thirty kilometres made their commute less stressful. The campus creates a synergized workspace that is also environmentally sustainable, using resources intelligently and efficiently. It successfully brings out the company's mission of 'add vitality to life' in offering facilities to employees that include convenience stores, a library, a food court, an occupational health centre, recreation zones and a daycare centre. HUL Campus uses green and energy-efficient building features such as rainwater harvesting, optimal use of glass and zero-waste water recycling concepts. The building design and landscaping has been done in a manner as to enhance the green cover in the campus. This concept is now considered standard; however, it was definitely forward looking a decade ago.

The main feature of the Campus is the 'Public Street' at the lower level of the office where the company provides amenities to its employees and also showcases its brands and service offerings—providing food, grocery retail stores and spaces for entertainment and breakout meetings. All this is plugged into an air-conditioned environment with its own cascading waterfall and glass walls looking out to the landscaped greenery. The Street is an apt metaphor, bringing the 'morphology of traditional Indian settlements inside the workplace, for a company whose revenues depend on its being in sync with its consumers. There are also listen-in kiosks with headsets where any employee can tune in to the Voice of the Consumer—recordings of calls made by consumers to the company's brand helplines and live video feeds from CCTVs located in mom-and-pop stores around the country, where one can glimpse a housewife engaged in comparison-shopping. This zone also acts as an incubation centre to test out new ideas, products and services before launching them into the market.

The workspace is a combination of open-plan cubicles and meeting zones that can be accessed through corridors and are set away from the cubicles to maintain privacy and calm. The sense of calm is reinforced through white interiors. 'We wanted the vibrancy to come from our people, the clothes they wear, and didn't want the environment to be overwhelmed by the furniture,' said Shaweta Pandey from the HUL corporate communications team in 2011[2]. The annexe has many other

---

[2] Vinay Kamath and Aarati Krishnan, 'Lever'-aging a better work-life balance', *Hindu Business Line*. Available at https://www.thehindubusinessline.com/specials/new-manager/lsquoLever-aging-a-better-work-life-balance/article20311354.ece. Updated on 29 July 2011.

facilities—it houses a training centre, a badminton court, a swanky gym, and a daycare centre which many working mothers and fathers really appreciate.

The shift to the new office was complemented with the encouragement to 'work where you are'—i.e., you could work anywhere within the campus (on the lawns, in the Street or even in the corridors) along with the more fundamental shift to let management-level staffers work out of home at least once a week or fortnight. All this was introduced when WFH was not even a known acronym.

As you can see from these two examples, Design Thinking is a powerful tool to define workspaces and direct work culture. There are several levels and scales at which design can influence corporate image and practice. Hence, corporate leaders should use it to the advantage of the company and its employees while maximizing benefits for all stakeholders but, at the same time, be aware of how it can affect the ecosystem too.

The address and location of the workspace definitely matters. This is why some business districts and hubs are more popular than others. Several factors can influence the choice of office location, but primarily it is dependent on the nature of business, the type of operation and the sector the company operates in.

The image of the office also makes a statement externally and internally and provides a cue to the vision of the company. Apart from the real estate values, the architecture of the building, the 'green' quotient and the efficiency of the floor plate are major factors influencing the choice of the building. Recent office architecture has tilted towards imagery, with an overdose of glass facades to blend in with the global look that is not necessarily the appropriate direction, especially in the context of energy conservation and appropriate identity-building.

It is always good to be in a location that is not very far from the airport (for larger corporations or service-based organizations), is extremely well-connected by public transport (metro, bus, train, expressways) and has housing facilities with various affordability levels so that employees find it convenient to reach and/or stay near the office. Key factors also include proximity to retail, restaurants and entertainment options apart from access to crèches and healthcare. All these factors contribute to making the daily workday routine a little less stressful.

These factors can also influence attrition as they attract prospective employees who choose organizations that offer fringe benefits. A well-located office near amenities and a diverse pool of housing, impact the status perceptions, convenience and commute timings of the employees. For the top management, apart from the above advantages, reserved parking is also a big perquisite.

Corporates also shift from legacy locations to consolidate operations, to redefine and reinvigorate internal culture. This is not merely a simple shift from one office to another, so the workplace should be carefully designed, planned, calibrated and executed to the advantage of all. Such shifts can have many negative impacts if not thought through properly.

The interior and environmental design of the workspace should imbibe the spirit of the organization and be in sync with its identity, values and culture. These should be identified well in advance and communicated and discussed in a collaborative manner with the designer to aid in the development of the layout—determining the space allocation, the hierarchy, the work processes, the requirements for privacy and any other specific needs of the organization. Constant communication with feedback can bring about updates to the design progressively. This communication-feedback process can create a feeling of participation among employees and reduce anxiety before the shift to a new workspace. I am a firm believer of the phrase

'Employees First, Customers Second'[3], the title of a popular book by Vineet Nayyar, the former CEO of HCL Technologies. This principle shifts the focus from customers to employees to create shared values that ultimately benefit the customers as well.

For a designer, every workplace project is a new challenge, as the philosophy, structure and aesthetics of the organization have to be integrated into a cohesive whole along with budgetary and practical considerations.

The workspace is an indicator of how an organization treats its employees. Different levels of staff utilize the workspace for different needs—the mid-level and top management see it as a space to perform tasks for productivity, while younger workers also see the workspace as a social space to interact with their co-workers.

Over the last decade, several concepts have been developed to improve productivity or save on real estate, reducing overhead costs. These include 'hot-desking' where employees who travel a lot are not assigned a specific desk but can choose from a pool of unallocated desks. In the Indian context, this leads to increased anxiety as the physical space of a defined desk is a symbol of job security. Many employees like to add their own personal touches to increase their feelings of comfort and belonging to their workspace as well as use it to communicate who they are to their co-workers. As mentioned earlier in the book, in India, the office structure and your office seat are also markers of your position in the hierarchy. There are status messages encoded in the placement and size of the allocated workspace and when there is no specific workplace, employees feel less important to the organization.

---

[3] Vineet Nayar, *Employees First, Customer Second: Turning Conventional Management Upside Down*, (USA: Harvard Business Review Press Edition, 2010).

Some offices have become cool places to be in, with a plethora of facilities such as cafes, work pods, nap areas, game rooms, free food and even concierge services. All this is done to retain talent and hook the employees into benefits that they cannot get elsewhere, especially in the IT and consulting sectors while other sectors tend to remain primarily functional.

COVID-19 has disrupted workspaces across the planet and accelerated the phenomenon of 'Work from Home', now commonly known as WFH. Its fundamental benefits of avoiding the stress of daily commutes and improved connections with the family have been overshadowed by feelings of isolation, lack of motivation and increased work hours. This seems to have contributed to a drop in productivity levels.

Some futurists in the US, as we know it, are writing obituaries for the office because COVID-19 has accelerated the acceptance of remote work, digitization and automation of processes. It is quite evident that globally, remote working is going to increase rapidly depending on the industry and nature of work. A large percentage of workers are preferring a permanent WFH status and are willing to change employers or move to what is now called the 'gig' workforce. Workers are calling it the 'Fourth Industrial Revolution' because it will fundamentally change industries and how people work. Several companies are using this churn to their advantage—saving time from unnecessary travel and meetings, reducing their real estate costs etc. Some researchers are also professing increased productivity and performance linked to improved mental health, better flexibility and the ability to hire the best talent across the world across time zones, while simultaneously reducing bias and increasing diversity.

In India, currently only about 10 per cent of the work force is engaged in 'computer-based office work' as against approximately 30 per cent in developed economies. The penetration of IT also depends on the digital integration of industries and work processes or tasks. It is quite clear that at least within the services industries (IT, Banking, Design etc.) organizations with higher levels of digitally enabled processes have adapted to COVID-19 much better than others. In parallel, the workspace environment and design will also have to be reincarnated. Lack of engagement levels during the epidemic has led to a reduction in the speed of decision-making and productivity. This has probably also led to reduced peer to peer learning due to lesser amounts of traditional collaboration among employees and working away from a professional environment. The physical distance between them means that almost all conversations have to be scheduled and purposeful, resulting in a lack of spontaneity and connection.

Most Indian homes are not designed for WFH. There are the issues of noise, technology gaps, family obligations and varied distractions. WFH also leads to work seeping into the personal life space and vice-versa in case timings and schedules are not adhered to properly or due to lack of private spaces. This is already leading to changes in the design of homes to adapt to WFH by incorporating improved Wi-Fi technology, creating private zones, with some even moving to larger homes where possible. There has also been a movement to the suburbs or to hometowns to be near family as well as to save on rent expenses.

Another trend that is emerging is 'Work Near Home' or WNH to improve work-life balance and increase productivity in a controlled office environment that is supportive of the work requirements but with safety and security measures, maintaining small bubbles of employees and key position holders in convenient locations. This has evolved to an increased use of co-working office spaces or smaller neighbourhood offices, where groups of employees may operate out of a satellite office most of the time and visit the main office periodically, in order to save on commute times or to have proximity to a specific client.

This seems to help in creating more cohesive work environments to encourage collaboration, concentration and focus, in addition to accommodating in-person meetings with clients and colleagues. Several organizations have also opted to let go of big office spaces, whether rented or owned, and have moved into a network of co-working centres and/or smaller neighbourhood offices in key locations.

The pandemic-initiated shift towards remote work has led to an unexpected yet profound change for the better in many households: fathers were more present at home, and most would now want to maintain some active roles in their children's lives as offices re-open. There are benefits to working fathers being more involved at home not just for their children and their partners (who traditionally bear an outsized burden when it comes to caregiving) but also for themselves. It is to be seen if working fathers will remain proactive in not reverting to pre-pandemic routines and behaviour. WFH has also impacted women negatively, with a bigger burden. They have had a tough time looking after the children while supervising online schooling from home and also increased household chores due to the entire family being at home all day as well.

With the risk from COVID-19 reducing or at least being managed better, getting back to the workspace has created a new paradigm and one size is not going to fit all. The myriad challenges ahead are probably going to generate many hybrid solutions, depending on the typology of work and service culture of the organization. These issues need to be addressed in a more humane manner.

Although Indian workers are getting used to WFH, a great majority still crave for the office environment and in-person interactions with colleagues as they have had an overdose of screen time with WFH. We are culturally more comfortable with personalized interactions rather than the virtual.

There is an enhanced need for vibrancy to ensure motivation for the office to re-start and emerge as a confluence for 'collective effervescence'. Collective effervescence is a sociological concept coined by Émile Durkheim[4]. According to Durkheim, a community or society may at times come together and simultaneously communicate the same thought and participate in the same action. This can enhance the feeling of belonging to the organization and purpose and engagement with one's work.

As for the architecture of the new office, spatial programming needs to support social distancing to define the layout, spaces, walkways, distinct islands of workstations and a variety of low-contact spaces. Openable windows along with ventilation features that control temperature, air flow and humidity more effectively along with enhanced filters and ionizers that help neutralize particulate matter, bacteria and virus cells, odorous gases, aerosols and VOCs + UV lights within ductwork are to be incorporated. Surfaces need to be resistant to contamination and easy to sanitize.

Natural textures of materials used in the design of offices convey a sense of being at 'home'; use of colours in floorings and ceilings can add energy to a workspace. Different pops of colour are a great way to separate space and improve navigation. This has to be woven with several features that redefine the open plan spaces—addition of more flexible meeting/workspaces, pods for privacy dovetailed with increased technology especially for video conferencing.

---

4 Emile Durkheim, *The Elementary Forms of the Religious Life*, (Dover Publications Inc., 2008).

There are several design philosophies that can be followed. The right one is usually a unique combination that is co-created specifically for the organization—a method I learned from management guru the late Dr C.K. Prahalad during the conception of Ginger Hotels for the Tata Group. It is a phase of introspection, discussion and collaboration while envisioning the growth of the organization in many ways—working on several innovations and improvements, major and minor at the same time, within the parameters of space, volume, budget and time.

Incubis Consultants has provided design-thinking consulting to several organizations to re-discover their legacies or create new ones while defining a future vision in the process of developing their businesses and workspaces. These include the following:

- A global hotel operator re-established its identity through the history of architecture, design and food trends over the last century, dovetailed with the life of its charismatic founder, and incorporated these within their hotel designs.
- An Indian IT incubator's collaborative workspace brought together layers of Indian crafts, mathematics (through proportions and diagrams) and the use of local materials in a modern metaphor, setting it apart from the banal global offices, which incorporate glass partitions and off-the-shelf modular workstations.
- A curated art programme for a global financial company that enlivened its new corporate office in India with the 'zeitgeist' or spirit of the nation marching ahead in the twenty-first century.

A few years ago, we shifted the Incubis studio from south Delhi to Gurugram. The shift was not easy as it disrupted travel routines for several employees. However, it provided us an opportunity to redefine and express our values and reinforce the work culture we wanted to nurture. The Incubis vision is to create spatial environments that are innovative and cost-effective, while using energy efficient and sustainable strategies. For the office, we chose a frugal design concept where we used materials in their natural state, recycled materials, re-used and up-cycled existing furniture. The layout portrays our democratic ethos while reflecting the energy and dynamism of a start-up environment. The studio conveys our vision to our employees and demonstrates our capabilities to clients with confidence.

Design thinking for workspaces, with its layers of metaphors, imagery, thought and architecture has the power to transform and define the corporate culture of an organization in a profound and humane manner. It is this belief that helps us provide innovative and diverse solutions to empower organizations to build empathetic and engaging communities.

Conclusion: One Fresh Start

As I conclude writing this book, I'm reminded of a story a client told me when I was still fresh and new to corporate work. He asked me if I knew how people in rural Punjab decide the weight limit for loading materials on donkeys. Of course, I didn't have a clue, even less than I had about the job I was trying to do. But I did know that marketing and advertising professionals thrive on these kinds of stories—our conversations meander through so many seemingly unrelated threads until we arrive at something that will stick and hopefully inspire our teams to create and our consumers to make a purchase. So, I was listening intently, waiting for the penny to drop.

Donkeys are made to stand with a brick under each leg, he said, and then loaded up till the bricks start to crack. That's how you decide the weight limit; the bricks tell you what the donkeys can't.

At the time, the story confused me. I was a little amused and wondered if I should also be a little insulted. Whom was the donkey meant to refer to? Was it me or was it our team? Was it the agency I worked for? Or was he referring to himself or the corporate world in general? I remained confused but I never forgot this story.

Today when it comes to mind again, I suddenly get it.

Culture is a living, breathing, evolving entity that shrinks and grows with people that make it and live within it. It's supposed to help us make sense of and cope with life, but it is no less complex and no less subjective. This book narrates some of our stories but each of us must make of it what we will.

The COVID-19 pandemic has disrupted our personal and professional worlds and destroyed whatever degrees of separation we had between them. The cracks in the bricks underlying our corporate culture, which were already visible earlier, now lie completely exposed. It appears we have reached our weight limit and it is time to reconsider our load.

I have to admit to a hint of disappointment because I was hoping for easy answers for myself. Yet, I find there are no such answers at work, just as there aren't any in life. The data and the experts can help us, perhaps even direct us, but the answers and efforts have to be our own. I think our tendency to look for easy solutions and adopt them without reflection is part of our problem. Our cultural norms are directions, but we often treat them as rigid rules, ones to be blindly conformed to as well as enforced. This cognitive laziness to follow the path set down for us rather than constantly evaluate and occasionally set our own pace seems to be our core issue.

I'm beginning to feel that I had probably set myself up for burnout even before my career started through the beliefs and values I had adopted, some willingly and some through conditioning.

I confess to deliberately becoming a workaholic. I chose the 'passion path' to do work that was engaging and meaningful to me, and I must admit that through my journey, I genuinely loved and enjoyed the work. Focusing on it helped me escape and distract myself from my pre-existing health condition. Working hard, as I have mentioned earlier, was a good excuse to avoid socializing rather than work on my poor social skills.

I found my work stress was easier to talk about to my limited inner circle than more personal stressors that I couldn't always understand and articulate. Work gave me an outlet to channelize my frustrations, and it helped me overcome some of my awkwardness. The confidence I built as I progressed in my career helped me want to tackle some of my personal issues. My motivation to do so was especially high when they interfered with my work. It was when my aggravated health condition started affecting my productivity that resolving it finally became a priority. I used my obsession with my job list to achieve my exercise goals because once a task was on my job list, I felt compelled to get it done.

So, the work itself has never been an issue. I appreciate and value all the lessons it has taught me, and I feel grateful for the empowerment it gave me, but my relationship with my work was and became increasingly toxic over the years. I realize that I made my work an unhealthy obsession. My entire self-worth was based on my career alone, so I felt every experience affected me much more closely and strongly than it should have. Everything felt personal, even if it was not meant to be.

Today we talk a lot about authenticity, but when I was growing up, the emphasis was on filling our roles. We tried to do things and adopt behaviours that helped us fit our roles better. My primary role, as I saw it, was that of a much-indulged daughter, and I feel, I consciously and unconsciously absorbed a lot of the ambition that my father had for me. I felt I needed to prove that I was worthy of all the opportunities and privileges he provided me. That ambition was made sharper by my need to prove myself as a woman following a career path, and more urgently, by my need to overcome and hide my health issues. I didn't want to fail, and I especially didn't want my gender or health to come in the way of my success.

On the surface, my early career choices seem to have been guided by my own desires rather than any cultural approval. Yet, I was not then, and am not now, immune to the cultural pressures we all face. I did feel the lack of money and status relative to my peers, which my advisors had warned me about when I chose to work in advertising. I did and still do want the concrete measures of success for their intrinsic value as well as to validate me and vindicate my choices.

At work, I feel I was always trying to fill a role—as an intern, as an account-managing executive, as an account planner, as a team player and as a team leader. I feel now that I was always trying too hard. And in this effort, I ruthlessly suppressed and repressed my feelings and tried to focus only on getting the job done well. As long as I could feel good about my work, I ignored my well-being in all other ways.

My internal reticence was further encouraged by the external status-consciousness, competitiveness and pressure to perform. Initially, I found it easier to buckle down and accept responsibility and criticism rather than challenge or assert myself with a boss, client or colleague. Over time, I learned to be more assertive for the sake of my work, but I still hesitated to ask for the rewards I wanted. I believed that if I just worked hard enough, they would come automatically.

Part of the reason I found it hard to be assertive about my needs and boundaries at work was because I was also excited by challenges and thought each one I crossed would make me feel more worthy and valued. I also worried that saying no to a boss would lead to rejection and to the end of my career, hopes and ambition. When I did learn to say no eventually, I found that saying no to myself was the real challenge and the first step I required before I said it to someone else. The same was true about the increments in salary and promotions I didn't ask for. I needed to convince myself that I deserved them before I could convince anyone else. Often, by the time I had convinced myself, the review season had passed and then I had to wait another year or more to ready myself to ask; only now, that hesitation was compounded with a feeling of being unappreciated and demotivated.

Antonio Damasio, a neuroscientist and professor of psychology, philosophy, and neurology, at the University of Southern California has written a book called *The Strange Order of Things: Life, Feeling and the Making of Culture*.[1] In this book, he shares his view that feelings play a key role in the making and changing of cultures. He writes that our cultural devices are meant to promote human well-being, but when they lead to human suffering instead, it's 'because they clash with simple as well as complex but non-deliberate homeostatic regulation.' Homeostasis 'ensures that life is regulated within a range that is not just compatible with survival but also conducive to flourishing, to a projection of life into the future of an organism or a species.' We are biologically programmed to seek a balance. If we eat too much, we feel full, and our appetite disappears. If we sleep too little, we feel tired and find it is difficult to focus and pay attention.

Kalyani Capoor recommends a balanced definition of success in Chapter 16, which shows us the criticality of balancing our various needs and investing our energy more effectively. This is the balance that I lacked and that I didn't think I needed when I decided to focus all my energy and time on work and ignore everything else. There was a decided lack of balance in my life and, eventually, no matter how much I loved my work, it was not enough to keep me from feeling the imbalance in my life and its effects. My well-being

---

[1] Antonio Damasio, *The Strange Order of Things: Life, Feeling and the Making of Culture*, (USA: Vintage Books, 2019).

depended on a far wider range of variables than I allowed myself to accept.

Strangely, the happiest I've been at work was during my three-month notice period before I took a break. None of my issues were resolved then but I felt lighter in the hope that they would be addressed. For the first time, I felt a detachment from my work and it enabled me to be productive and effective without being stressed and anxious. I was able to leave the office on time without guilt, say no to extra work without fear and felt all my work and personal interactions were more authentic and engaging. I woke up in the morning feeling content and safe, with that 'vibrant, bouncy feeling' accompanying me to work that R.R. Nair mentions in Chapter 18.

My friends and mentors had told me over the years that I needed to detach myself from my work, but I didn't really understand exactly what they meant. It was only possible after I was able to let go of the urgent, impatient ambition that had constantly nagged at me.

This research project and book was born out of my feelings at that stage in my life. I felt that a break would help me correct the imbalance, but I also worried that I might go to the other extreme without the discipline of a job and its demands. I feared that when I returned to a corporate job, I might regress and fall back into my pattern and end up out of balance again. I needed to work on myself for sure, but to do that, I also needed some answers, some clarity and some sense of direction to better understand the corporate world. This project has uncovered some expected and unexpected insights, and my panel of experts has provided us with a map and some sense of direction. I realize now just how critical it is that we keep working on ourselves along the way.

Experts on work improvement and organizational design, Liz Fosslien and Mollie West Duffy say, 'Emotional culture is built on emotional norms, the unspoken rules that dictate what you're allowed to feel and express.'[2] I find emotions contagious and that may be why they play such an important role in building and perpetuating culture.

I always worked better in those environments where bosses and colleagues were optimistic, encouraging and empowering. Since my self-belief was low, I needed others to show faith in me. That elevated my happiness at work, which, however, also varied with the narrative I told myself. When I allowed myself to believe that I was where I deserved to be, that I was working well and producing results, I felt energetic, motivated and satisfied. When I let myself believe that I was out of my depth, stuck or unappreciated, I felt lethargic, demotivated and unhappy. When environments, bosses and colleagues were pessimistic, discouraging and controlling, it fed into my negative self-talk.

While I've always used my feelings to guide me in my career choices, I have also censored them when I was at work with filters of my own and that of the workplace culture as I perceived it. I immersed myself in working hard, putting my head down and ignoring the things I didn't like or didn't get. But that was never enough.

When I became a team leader, I found I couldn't ignore the office gossip and office politics anymore, but I lacked the experience and skills to navigate them. I had not tracked the undercurrents and alliances and was not in a position where I could take the time to learn. My wilful blindness was too entrenched by then. I realize now that idealism needs to be tempered with practicality—another balance that was missing for me.

---

2 Liz Fosslien and Mollie West Duffy, *No Hard Feelings: Emotions at Work and How They Help Us Succeed*, (Portfolio Penguin, 2019).

When some parts of our lives develop cracks, they can and do affect our ability to shoulder the weight of our work. We need the right amount of weight so that we can keep our balance, and it is this sense of balance that enables our best efforts at work. Now that I have made some efforts to achieve it, I know that it is not a stable place for me but a series of trade-offs. I choose to invest my time and energy like a balanced investment portfolio. Some days I may tilt towards work, on others, get inclined to exercise or spend time with family, but together they all add up to create a balance. I need to be more alert, aware and deliberate to make it work, to decide for myself and make my own choices rather than take the easy way of copying what someone else chooses for themselves.

Will I be able to sustain this? I don't know, but I won't ever know if I don't try, mindful of the fact that I am always going to be a work-in-progress and never reach some perfectionist ideal.

It's scary to admit to not having a blueprint for our careers. We're expected to know not just what we want from our careers right now but also where we expect to be one or three or five years from now. It's not just job interviewers who ask this of us but our bosses, families and community ask us as well and yet, the prepared answers we have are not nuanced or fine-tuned to ourselves but skewed to what we think they need to hear. Our anxiety about failing their judgment leads us to judge ourselves much too harshly, making us conform instead to the kind of things we ought to be questioning. We imagine unrealistic perfectionist goals and then beat ourselves up in the attempt to get there. If we can be more real and have empathy for ourselves, we might find it easier and more organic to extend it to others.

While this book and the research project behind it have not covered cases of ethical breaches, I feel I can now see how some poor decisions can be made despite good intentions. A culture that discourages questioning status and authority, our preference for looking for easy directions and competitive advancement and leaders put under tremendous pressure for short-term performance are not conducive to ethical behaviour. We don't give ourselves and/or are not given the time to reflect, understand and appreciate the nuances of ethics in the duress to act quickly. I find some advocates of business ethics as idealistic as I am and perhaps that makes us too harsh in our outlook and judgement. The COVID-19 situation shows this starkly. It's easy to tell a business that they must put employee welfare over business interests but if the business cannot be sustained, the employees will suffer anyway. Leaders have been trying but perhaps, they might do better if ethical custodians were more inclined to listen to their struggles with empathy and offer more customized, nuanced guidance to help them balance their conflicting demands.

The pandemic has taught us that we cannot resist change forever. Either we choose to adapt, or we will be forced to do so by sudden disruptions. The people and organizations that had already experimented with or adopted technology platforms and remote working were better placed to handle the lockdowns than the ones who hadn't. Do we want to wait till we are compelled to change, or do we want to be prepared?

We Indians tend to care too much about what other people think and too little for our own experiences. Indian philosophy says, the world is an illusion, and yet we let it shape and mould us when we should be the ones shaping and moulding it. I feel we do have a choice and we do play a part in shaping our work environment and corporate culture.

I also believe that we cannot change culture forcefully by shaming and demanding change. We can influence cultural change by changing ourselves, by role modelling the behaviour we wish to see as commonplace and by deliberately choosing what we value rather than falling blindly in line with the values enforced by our deeply entrenched cultural codes.

So even though there is no immediate sense of closure through an easy solution, I feel there is potential for change because I do understand my career trajectory better now and also have a clearer sense of where I have taken wrong turns or misplayed the corporate game.

Let's become more deliberate and conscious in taking the time to reflect on what we accept, what we demand and the boundaries we want to set to protect our health, our relationships and the quality of our lives. Defining and revising our goals and priorities has to be an on-going process because our needs and priorities will keep changing. We need to be more aware, reflective and open to continuous learning. Every decision we make for ourselves could be inspiring and contagious or it could provoke judgement, discouragement and exclusion. We need to choose for ourselves what we want and can be happy with, and we need to allow some flexibility for those who may choose differently.

Our choices are ours to make. Our minds are ours to change. And the Indian corporate culture will evolve as we do.

Acknowledgements

First of all, I would like to thank all the respondents who took time out of their busy schedules to participate in the research and generously shared their personal experiences and learnings with me—those who participated in the formal research organized by Quantum Consumer Solutions, those who answered my online surveys and polls and those who read some of my initial writing on LinkedIn and reached out to me to share their reactions and stories.

Anjana Pillai and her team at Quantum Consumer Solutions understood and translated my vision for this book into a viable research design. My heartfelt thanks to everyone who planned and analysed the research and did the fieldwork, moderation, transcription and analysis.

The personal and the professional realms overlap in myriad ways, and I feel fortunate that I have personal connections with incredibly talented, experienced and credible professionals who have inspired, encouraged and actively participated in my project. While this book has taken four years to plan, research and write, the idea emerged, incubated and evolved over a much longer period, over my whole career and perhaps even before then.

Some of the curiosity may be credited to my father, Uday Khanna, whose corporate career and network has benefitted me as I was growing up and who has also been very supportive of this project. Much of the clarity belongs to my mamu and mami, Ashok and Kalyani Capoor, who have been my mentors, guides and emotional support system, from way before I studied management, throughout my career and life since then. So much of my inspiration, motivation and insights have come out of conversations with them that I feel this book is as much theirs as it is mine.

I have been lucky that I have had R.R. Nair's advice and guidance over much of my life. He has been especially involved in the development of this book and helped me understand and craft much of its content. Rohit Krishan Gulati brought an invaluable outsider's perspective to the research insights, and I am especially appreciative of his steady contributions despite his tough experiences with COVID-19.

I met my best friends, Deepika Beniwal and Minaxi Indra, at IIM Bangalore and we have been a part of each other's life–career journeys for two decades and counting. They have been my champions and sounding boards for this book, as with all other things, and have helped me always to challenge, change and expand my perspective.

Anjum Hasan, Eshwar Sundaresan and Zac O'Yeah lead an impactful writing workshop called Bangalore's World-Famous Semi-Deluxe Writing Program in collaboration with Shoonya, a non-profit, multi-arts centre. I was fortunate to be selected for the program in August 2019, and I would like to thank all the instructors, the coordinator, Avinash, the staff at Shoonya and my fellow participants, especially my writing buddy, Saranya Subramanian, for their guidance and support, which taught me to challenge myself and work much harder on my writing ability. I am especially grateful for their feedback and criticism when I presented an inarticulate, incoherent plan for this book, which forced me to focus on finding my clarity and motivated me to do all the necessary groundwork for it.

This book owes a great deal to its fairy godfather, Sandip Ghose, who took great interest in connecting me with many people who contributed to it and towards getting it published. Thank you to Tarini Uppal for reading and reviewing my book proposal and for forwarding it to Shreya Punj, who took it forward and is the primary editor of this book. I am so grateful to Shreya, for supporting, encouraging and introducing me to the world of publishing, and to Sudisha Mukherji for helping me navigate the legalese of it. Thank you to the entire team at Penguin Random House India, especially Shaoni Mukherjee for her painstaking copy editing and Meru Gokhale for her leadership of the editorial team as well as Aparna Kumar and Chirag Thakkar for stepping into the editorial role in their turn. I'm also grateful to the marketing and distribution teams at Penguin for putting their might behind my first book.

I have found incredible generosity when connecting with writers and published authors as they have been willing to take the time to discuss, debate and critique my initial work, even with the most tenuous of interpersonal links. All of them shared with me useful tips on improving writing skills, maintaining discipline, finding clarity, pitching to publishers and book marketing.

Aarti Kelshikar (author of *How India Works: Making Sense of a Complex Culture*), Chitra Narayanan (editorial consultant at *The Hindu Business Line* and author of *From Oberoi to Oyo*), Eshwar Sundaresan (author of *Behind the Silicon Mask* and *Bangalored*), Rajesh Srivastava (author of *The New Rules of Business* and *The 10 New Life-changing Skills*) and Vikram Khanna (associate editor at *The Straits Times*, Singapore) reviewed my book proposal, and I credit their feedback for its eventual success.

I want to thank those who allowed me to quote their opinions directly in this book: Minaxi Indra, Rajesh Gangwani, Smitha Shetty and Jasravee Kaur Chandra. Additional thanks to Jasravee for featuring me in her podcast on branding and marketing, 'Jagged with Jasravee', and to Smitha for interviewing me for her coaching series on the Facebook group, Women from IIM Worldwide.

Amisha Bahl Chawla and Shyam Chawla created and produced beautiful animation videos to promote my articles and this book. Amisha also operates my YouTube channel and is my guru on digital marketing. I'm so grateful for their incredible talent, professionalism and our long-standing friendship.

Vinita Bali agreed to write the foreword for this book on short notice, even as she was recovering from illness and dealing with a tremendous backlog of work. I am thankful for her time and effort as well as for her encouragement over the years.

I'd also like to thank everyone who shared their interest and feedback on the idea of this book and on my initial writings via conversations, emails and comments on LinkedIn and Whatsapp for helping me validate, evolve and consolidate my work. I've listed the names below in alphabetic order and apologize to anyone I may have missed. I have a tricky memory, so feel free to embarrass me for it, as I deserve.

Aarti Sood, Aditya Puri, Aditya Somani, Akhil Gupta, Alka Kakar, Alka Puri, Amar Kampani, Amol Sandil, Amulya Rao, Andita Rao, Anita Puri, Anjali Puri, Anumita Ghosh, Arya Vasudevan, Asha Nehemiah, Ashita Gulati, Ashok Barat, Bharat Puri, Binod K. Maitin, Deepa Khanna, Deepak Sapra, Dinesh Kapoor, Harsh Goenka, Harshbeena Zaveri, Indrani Bhuyan, John Alexander, K.N. Thejavathy, Krish Shankar, Kiran Mehta, Krishna Prasad, Madhura Krishnaswamy, Manju Sanghrajka, Meena Kaushik, Michele Suradkar, Monika Khanna Gulati, Muktesh Pant, Naveen Kshatriya, Neeti Gupta,

Netra Ramachandran, Nisha Venugopalan, Nitya Khanna, Piyush Pandey, Poonam Thapar, Prasad Chandran, Priya Lobo, R. Gopalakrishnan, Radhika Tulsian Gulati, Rahul Malhotra, Rajeev Thapar, Rajnish Mehra, Ranjit Shahani, Ravindra Dhariwal, Renu Khanna Gulati, Sachid Madan, Sanjiv Mehta, Santrupt Misra, Saroj Kakar, Shilpa Rangaswamy, Shilpi Thapar Jaisingh, Shruthi Kubair Ranga, Steve Correa, Sumeer Mathur, Sundeep Kakar, Susan Mathen, Tanvi Rella, Tina Sachdev, Thillai Ganesh Chelian, Urvashi Tandon, Vandana Joshi, Vigyan Verma, Vikram Kaushik, Vijay Parathasarathy, Vivek Pai, Zara Alam Khan-Nygård.

Ravitej Rao of CrestLaw Partners and Ajitha G.S., managing editor at Westland Publications, answered my initial queries about copyright and the publishing process, without which I may have been too intimidated to start this journey. And special thanks to M. Vallinayagam, Rajanish Putt and Mimi Paratha Sarathy and their team at Sinhasi Consultants for taking on my confused financial assets and putting them in order to make both my break and this book possible.

Everyone I have ever worked with during my career has been part of my learning, growth and development to this point. There are too many names to list here but I would like to mention my favourite boss/mentors—Preethi Maroli and Pete Heskett. They showed me that a great working environment and team culture could be created and nurtured even with a diverse team spread across the globe, intense pressure to perform and several other constraints.

And finally, thank you, dear readers, for buying this book. I hope you get some insights and ideas from it so you can shape our corporate culture to benefit and enrich all our lives.